To Marie
my friend.
Here's looking at life
Dick Walliat
Happy Trails

Courage To Change The Things I Can

The Remarkable Texas Story of Richard "Dick" Wallrath

By James Pomerantz

This book is available in quantity for special discounts for groups or organizations. For further information, contact: Bandana Books, LLC 847-441-0903 847-441-8139 fax
www.bandanabooks.com

Printed in the USA
ISBN 1-59975-231-X

Contents

A Message From Dick Wallrath

Author's note

Foreword by Texas Governor Rick Perry

Foreword by United States Senator Kay Bailey Hutchison, R-Texas

Foreword by P. Michael Wells

President and CEO/Houston Livestock Show and Rodeo

Foreword by Richard "Tres" Kleberg

From the legendary King Ranch Family

Chairman of the Board / San Antonio Stock Show and Rodeo

Foreword by former PRCA World Champion Bull Rider Bobby Steiner

Bastrop, Texas

Cast of Characters

Chapters;

A Message From Dick Wallrath

The purpose of this book is to hopefully motivate people to succeed in life.

Positive thinking is not an aberration. Positive energy is a choice. You can chose to move forward with enthusiasm and accept the God within all of us. Success will follow the outstretched hand of generosity. My life has come full circle in my agreement with a power greater than I.

Sobering up in Galena Park, Texas and finding myself in a hopeless state of mind and body, I began to think that my life had been wasted. I had to start from zero. Through a twelve step program, I was able to inventory my past life which was a total loss. I found my long and short points. With God's help, I was able to cultivate the good and positive aspects of my life and I was able to push past the negative points.

I only had a high school education and was never able to go to college. I felt like there were two separate individuals living inside my body. There was the "no good son-of-a-gun" when I was drinking and there was the man I sought to become today. I was given a copy of "Think and Grow Rich" by Napolean Hill. The book stressed goals, self-discipline and time limits to success. I knew that if I could stop drinking, I could reach my goals. By not drinking one day at a time and two hands full of faith, it has been possible for me to succeed in life. God has blessed me with thirty-eight years of sobriety and counting.

God has blessed me with an abundance of friends. God has placed me in a position to meet many young people and to help them get on a path to success with education, the key that will help them unlock the door to their future.

The difference between success and failure is that you make more right decisions than wrong ones. Rockefeller was asked what it took to be successful and he replied that it took three things. #1. Figure out what you want. #2. Figure out what you are willing to give up to get what you want. #3. Get two hands full and get it on.

I am a firm believer that you have to give to receive. Though my business and professional life appeared to be successful, I give God all the credit for the good things that have occurred and I have taken credit for all the mess-ups. For all the success, I am most grateful to God for all the blessings.

Personally, as a father, I have only been fifty percent. I have two children that I am close to and I thank God for them. I have two other children that have absolutely nothing to do with me and I personally feel that as a father, I failed them. However, I still love each of them with an unconditional love. I have one daughter that is deceased and I feel that a part of me died with her. I have to use the serenity prayer in times of need...God grant me the serenity to accept the things I cannot change, the courage to change the things I can and the wisdom to know thew difference.

I hope this book will find its way to someone full of self-pity and resentment, someone who feels like a real loser. I pray the book may be a path out of darkness to the light of living and open the door to a glorious future. This book is for anyone with the courage to get two hands full and get it on. Abandon yourself to God as you understand God. Clear away the wreckage of your past, give freely of what you find and surely you will meet some of us as you trudge the road to a happy destiny. May God bless you and keep you until then.

Author's Note

January 16, 2005

I was summoned to Centerville, Texas to meet the man I would be writing about. The subject had been quite intriguing. My job would be to hang out in Texas and gather information about a recovered alcoholic (thirty-eight years and counting). Dick Wallrath was married with a child when he graduated high school. With five kids, no job and an appetite for nearly a quart of whiskey per day, Dick Wallrath finally caught sight of the man he had become. This was not the man his parents raised. The ensuing epiphany began a path that would lead to sobriety, great success in business and a philanthropic determination to share his good fortune with young people throughout the state of Texas. I had to write a book about a guy who paid $600,001.00 for one steer named Popcorn. I flew into the Dallas/Fort Worth airport, my least favorite airport of note. The drive to Centerville was less than three hours. Centerville is located halfway between Houston and Dallas. Centerville boasts a population of 903. A small café with great breakfast fare is affectionately referred to as the "Choke and Puke." I had been instructed to turn right at the courthouse and proceeded two miles to the entrance of the ranch.

Wallrath Champion Ranch, owned by Richard "Dick" Wallrath, is a six-thousand plus acre cattle ranch in Central Texas, sitting some forty minutes north of the Texas State Prison at Huntsville. The ranch boasts of twenty-five miles of paved roads, fourteen oil wells, a full-sized rodeo arena, two bunkhouses accommodating twenty people and many other dwellings including an old fashioned Texas roadhouse saloon. There are smokehouses, private lakes, twenty-five hundred head of cattle and a prized string of mares, colts, studs and geldings. I pulled into the ranch and immediately into a small parking lot adjacent to the offices for the ranch. Behind the office complex I could see a half dozen buffalo undisturbed by the arriving vehicles. Scattered herds of Brangus cattle dotted the rolling pastures for as far as the eye could see. Dick Wallrath pulled into the lot at precisely the same time. He drove a brand new Cadillac Escalade pick-up, white with gold trim. A twelve-gauge shotgun adorned the dashboard, loaded and clipped next to a digital GPS screen. Dick got out of the truck and we shook hands. Richard Wallrath dressed well, but make no mistake about it, dressed to leave no doubt about where he was from. From the pearly white Stetson to the embroidered denim shirt, Texas erupted from every article of clothing, every choppy step and every word that rolled out of his mouth.

" I expected an intellectual dressed in a three piece suit." Wallrath announced on our first meeting. "You gotta be from New York? Right?"

He already knew that I was from Chicago. He knew what I looked like from the picture on my last book. It didn't matter. The man told me that he was surprised to meet an author wearing jeans, a black t-shirt, Luccese boots and a Bob Berg belt buckle. We walked into the office and Dick sat behind his desk. He pulled up his jeans and pulled a titanium '38 revolver from his boot holster.

" I may be seventy-something years old, but no sonofabitch is going to carjack my Escalade." Wallrath smiled and spun the pistol around. I wondered what might happen if I wrote a bad book. However, I knew I liked this guy from the moment I met him.

Texas is an enigma to those from outside the state and a sanctuary to those calling Texas home. Texans neither feel the need to explain the state to outsiders nor the obligation to justify the juxtaposition of each separatist connotation associated with Texas. The hubristic nature of a Texan is not born from a desire to be close to the whimsical blather filling the nation's airways, but "Texas Pride" is born from a place known as the symbol for the ultimate sacrifice for freedom. The Alamo is not a forgotten legend in Texas. It is not a time to remember only when Hollywood deems it necessary to fabricate another version. Men and women in Texas build their lives with long memories. They seek to uphold the history from those hallowed grounds in San Antonio. The final assault came on March 6, 1836. The Texians and Tejanos held out for 13 days against Santa Anna's army, a siege of thousands against an army of less than two hundred defenders inside the Alamo. Texans carry on the tradition of struggle and revel when the odds are greatest not to succeed. Overcoming great odds in Texas is not a deterrent, but a birthright. Dick Wallrath is a Texas mindset. Marred with a bleak future, fully self-induced, Mr. Wallrath not only faced his weaknesses head on, he learned to share the wisdom and strength that success rendered.

Someone once said…

"Two children were singled out for a study. The pessimistic child was placed in a room full of toys, alone for an hour. The optimistic child was placed in a room full of horse manure for an hour. After an hour, the door was opened to the room with the pessimistic child. All the toys were broken and the child sat on the floor crying. Next, the door was opened to the room with the optimistic child. The optimistic child was playing in the horse manure and smiling. The question was asked, why? The child replied, with that much horse shit, there had to be a pony in there somewhere."

There is nothing coincidental about a state that has produced the likes of President George H. Bush, President George W. Bush, Lance Armstrong, Ty Murray, President Lyndon Baines Johnson, President Dwight Eisenhower, Ernie Banks, A.J. Foyt, George Foreman, Howard Hughes, Waylon Jennings, Steve Martin, Fleet Admiral Chester Nimitz, Oliver North U.S. Congresswoman Barbara Jordan, George Jones, Kris Kristofferson, Rafer Johnson, Lee Trevino, Tanya

Tucker, Stevie Ray Vaughan and George Strait. What runs common among these names is a will to overcome odds and the determination to focus on clear goals. Dick Wallrath may not sit inside a Hall of Fame associated with sports, music or politics, but Mr. Wallrath has taken a page from Texas lore and the passage is nothing short of inspirational and magical. Down here in Texas, these folks know how to take responsibility for their own actions, a concept nationally forgotten and sorely missed. The life experiences of Dick Wallrath are not intended to preach about the acquisition of wealth, but are intended to assign culpability to one's plight and assess the intention to change. We are not prisoners. We are failing practitioners.

There have been many stories written about men and women reared in poverty and humble beginnings that have risen to great wealth and stature. Walter Payton wrote, just before he passed away, that we must make every day count for something. We must appreciate every moment because it may be the last time we are able to exist within that moment. Walter set his sights high and believed in his ability to reach those lofty heights. Believe in yourself, Payton spoke of, because if you don't, no one else will. Dick Wallrath and Walter Payton have more than one common thread. Setbacks and regrets are roadkill. Perceive where it is you want to be and get there. "Begin with the end in mind. Live every day to its fullest and be as gracious as you can be".

God grant me the serenity

To accept the things I cannot change;

Courage to change the things I can;

And wisdom to know the difference.

Reinhold Niebuhr

Let's go meet Dick Wallrath.

Foreword by Texas Governor Rick Perry

July 9, 2005

The story of Dick Wallrath is one of a man who understands one of life's great truisms: that our blessings are never made full until shared with others. Dick Wallrath has not only led a successful life, but a significant life, sharing the blessings of his successful business to enrich the lives of many in need. He has poured his heart and soul into providing youth opportunity through education. He has reached an entire generation, instilling values that will last a lifetime, self-discipline, personal responsibility, love and charity. And he has touched none more than those who belong to 4H and Future Farmers of America.

I have vivid memories as a young boy in 4H and FFA. When I came home from school, waiting in the wings wasn't a game boy, but instead Big Boy, my club calf. Big Boy required daily attention. He needed to be fed, groomed and washed. I even had to teach him how to walk. So this eighty pound, rail-thin, nine year-old tied that club calf of several times his weight to a toolbar on a John Deere tractor, and away we went. Along with the chores required by my parents every day, Big Boy helped teach me about taking responsibility, a lesson 4H and FFA teach thousands of young men and women every year.

Self-discipline, personal responsibility, perseverance and trustworthiness, these are the traits taught by 4H and FFA, and the traits that define Dick Wallrath. Dick was drawn to these organizations and the youth who benefit from them because of these very reasons. No single person or company has donated more money to the Houston Livestock Show and Rodeo than Dick Wallrath. The founder of Champion Window Company, Dick has transformed this thirty-five year entrepreneurial endeavor as a mechanism to shower his generosity on youth, especially those who participate in agricultural shows and organizations.

He has also stepped into the gap for those facing healthcare emergencies, including paying for the medical bills of employees' family members and plastic surgery for a disfigured child with no other means to receive healing medicine. Dick has generously helped young Texans go to college, paying tuition bills many could never afford on their own.

Whether providing money for education or medical costs, six-figure bids at livestock shows that benefit our youth, or meeting the needs of wayward children through the establishment of Boy's Country in Hockley, Texas, Dick Wallrath and Patsy Murphy have contributed immensely to Texas and her people.

Perhaps nothing explains his generosity more than the realization he came to many decades ago that he was but one mortal sinner in need of redemption. A recovering alcoholic, Dick Wallrath has found redemption through the grace of God. And he knows we have but one opportunity to make an eternal difference, one life to give glory to God by serving Him and serving others. And that he has done to the benefit of thousands and to the inspiration of many more. He is a living legend whose life is an enduring lesson: everything we have been blessed with and given is not intended for our eternal keeping, but to be shared with others. If we do that, we will live lives enriched by more than silver and gold...lives enriched by eternal, divine purpose.

Governor Rick Perry

Republican

State of Texas

Foreword by Senator Kay Bailey Hutchison, R-Texas

July 8, 2005

Generosity is a tradition in Texas and Dick Wallrath embodies this timeless trait. He has a heart as big as Texas and has shared his success with those less fortunate. Dick has a passion for education and supports it through livestock auctions in Houston, San Antonio and Austin. These shows provide scholarship funds for college bound students.

Dick Wallrath is an exemplary role model, mentor and philanthropist. He has fulfilled the American dream and, through his generosity, he has influenced the lives of many young persons who will be the future leaders in our community. His life story and his contributions have inspired others to succeed. This is a tremendous legacy to share with others.

United States Senator Kay Bailey Hutchison

Republican-Texas

Foreword...

June 20, 2005

Through the years of working with Dick Wallrath, a warm and lasting friendship has developed. His life story has been an inspiration to me and countless others.

No one has been more identified with the mission of the Houston Livestock Show and Rodeo for helping the young people of Texas than Dick Wallrath! He is the single all-time high buyer at our Junior Market Steer Auction with the record for a single purchase of $600,001 and total accumulated purchases in excess of $3,000,000. Dick truly is committed to helping make a major difference in the lives of these young men and women. He IS the definition of "generosity".

P. Michael Wells

President and CEO

Houston Livestock Show and Rodeo

Foreword...

April 28, 2005

Dick Wallrath is a unique blend of cowboy and businessman, with a generous and giving heart that reaches out to our youth. He is a fiercely loyal and dedicated friend. Dick believes that one of the keys to our future is the education of our youth. He has been blessed with success, and continues to find ways of sharing it with others.

Richard M. "Tres" Kleberg, III

From the legendary King Ranch family, Kingsville, Texas

Chairman of the Board

San Antonio Livestock Exposition, Inc.

San Antonio Stock Show and Rodeo

San Antonio, Texas

Foreword…

June 1, 2005

Dick Wallrath is a no bullshit guy. He says what he means and he means what he says. Not only is he my favorite philanthropist, but someone I can always count on. He is also my friend.

Bobby Steiner

Bastrop, Texas

Former PRCA World Champion Bull Rider

Father to 2002 PRCA World Champion Steer Wrestler Sid Steiner and Country Music recording artist Tommy Shane Steiner.

Cast of Characters...

Richard "Dick" Wallrath, the source for our story.

Patsy Murphy, Dick's partner for life, lover, best friend, confidant, soul mate, etc.

Michael Richard Wallrath, Dick's oldest son.

Pamela Kay Dolenz, Dick's daughter.

Joni Jean Matthews, Dick's daughter.

Daniel Dwight Wallrath, Dick's son.

Dina (Deede) Denise Robertson, Dick's youngest daughter (deceased).

Gary Robertson, Dina's husband, Alexander's father.

Alexander Robertson, Gary and Dina's son, Dick's grandson.

Garrett, Justin, Pam's children, Dick's grandchildren.

Matt, Kati, Joni's children, Dick's grandchildren.

Telina, Mark, Brande, Shelley (deceased), Michael's children, Dick's grandchildren.

Jereme, Aaron, Danny's children, Dick's grandchildren.

Ruth Julia Hetrick Wallrath, Dick's mother.

Frederick Wallrath, Dick's father.

Eva Jo White, Dicks' sister.

Betty Wallrath, Dick's first wife (divorced).

Texas Governor Rick Perry, friend.

Ralph Zuckerberg, CEO-Champion Window, business partner and friend.

Andy and Pat Vavra, business associates and friends.

Robert Adam, attorney and friend.

Bobby Steiner, Former PRCA World Champion Bull Rider, friend and business associate.

Michael Wells, President-Houston Stock Show and Rodeo, friend.

Aaron Alejandro, Executive Director-Texas FFA Foundation, friend and advisor.

James Reeves, Executive Director-Texas 4-H Clubs, friend and advisor.

Dr. Phil Leggett, General Surgeon, personal physician and friend.

Tuffy Loftin, Champion Ranch manager and friend.

Senator Kay Bailey Hutchison, United States Senator from Texas and friend.

Richard "Tres" Kleberg, Chairman of the Board-San Antonio Stock Show and Rodeo and friend.

CHAPTER 1

Chapter One...Life Had Become Unmanageable, It Couldn't Be Mine.

Frederick Wallrath had danced with the bell of success. Fred Wallrath was not a rich man by the standards of Wall Street or the Texas oil fields, but there was the sweet smell of success from the fruits of his farm labor. The depression threw a curve into Frederick Wallrath's life and he never could quite hit that curve. Richard "Dick" Wallrath was born in 1930. He was the last of six children. Fred was a strict German man, small in stature, but big on the moral character of his children. There were two sides of the fence and he never wanted to catch any of his children on the wrong side of the fence.

Ruth Julia Hetrick Wallrath was a very small Dutch woman, an immaculate homemaker and Dick's mother. Ruth saw the good in everyone. While the family had fallen back into poverty after the Depression, Frederick had a difficult time accepting his newfound misfortune. Clouded inside a permanent mental depression, Frederick Wallrath never adjusted to the sharecropper lifestyle again. The farm grew some corn, wheat and beans. Milk supplemented the farm income. Fred killed the family meat supply. Hogs slaughtered were sugar cured. The hams were wrapped in newspapers with brown sugar and red pepper. The unmistakable smell of bacon and eggs with fresh biscuits and gravy in the morning was the staple for the Wallrath farm.

The old, two-story farmhouse had no indoor plumbing or electricity until Dick was in the eighth grade. Homework was done by kerosene lamp. There were no lights in the barn. All work after dark was done by lantern and Fred insisted that his children be more than aware of the fire hazards presented by the lanterns.

Dick Wallrath: We had chamber pots in all the bedrooms. Mother would empty those chamber pots every morning, but if you had to do some serious movement, then you had to get your ass outside to the outhouse. When the wintertime took a bite out of the air, we'd ball up inside until we had to burst. That damned outhouse just kept gettin' further and further away. The hole would fill up and my dad would move the sonofabitch farther away from the house. Two things stick out in my mind about my mother. The first, is when we got the indoor plumbing and the electricity in our house. Mother didn't have to mess with those chamber pots. She never complained but I knew the sun had come up higher on the day those pots found a home in the corner of the barn. My other memory of my mother that lives in the front of my mind is the way my success tickled her to death. My father died when in 1978, but my mother lived until 1994 and she was able to enjoy some of the financial success that Champion Windows produced. I had an interest in a plane for a time and I used to ask mother if she wanted to go to Mexico. She would perk up and with a huge smile and tell me to get the plane ready! Hell, she was asleep before the thing got off the ground. I'd take her to the Princess Hotel in Acapulco, Mexico. She'd line up pedicures, manicures, facials, massages and hair salon appointments. I guess she tried to make up for the years that those appointments were never a thought in her mind. I am so glad that she was able to enjoy some those perks before she died.

Coal stoves, leather razor straps and chores before and after school were the stereotypical rural foundation that may not have won any present day parent of the year awards, but nevertheless proved to be the backbone of a nation emerging from the depths of a depression. Fred Wallrath raised his son to respect authority and it did not take too many appointments with the belt strap to drive home a point. Alcohol was not present in the Wallrath home except for an occasional dip during the holidays. The whippings were not drunken extensions of some bottled up rage. The whippings were simple solutions to rural discipline issues. Fred Wallrath didn't call for a timeout or a Ritalin tablet.

Dick Wallrath did not invent the glue in his past. The ties to another era were still vibrant within those defined by a tougher standard of discipline. Children raised in rural America were not products of the media. The images indelible in their minds were born from religion and the rigid structure of farm life. School, church, chores and meals were the cornerstones of life. Personalities and character did not come from a television or the outside influence of a record producer. Dick Wallrath first encountered the outside world with Fred's acquisition of a radio in 1936 or 1937. The farm was still without electricity. Fred would bring in the battery from the vintage Chevrolet in the driveway.

Dick Wallrath: I know for a fact that the first introduction to a celebrity that I had was with President Roosevelt and his inaugural address carried live on radio. Hell, I'm not even sure that it was an inaugural address, but it was the speech where Roosevelt told Americans that the only thing to fear is fear itself. Man, how powerful is that today? It stayed with me and is still with me today. I remember when I first bought a bicycle. I was twelve years old. There were hardly any males around because of the war. I was able to make a man's wages for the work around the farms of our neighbors. There were no men around, so the work was plentiful and lucrative for those days. After I completed everything I had to do at my house, I would go to work for the neighbors. My dad had a friend who was able to secure a bicycle for me. During the war, that was next to impossible. I finally got my new bicycle. I had worked my ass off for that bicycle and I paid for every penny of that thing. I rode it to the next town to show it off to all my friends. Coming home in the dark, damned if I didn't run that thing into a parked car. I carried my new bicycle home in a shopping bag. I learned early on that success was going to come with some baggage. It would take some years before I figured out that all the baggage in the world was easy to acquire, but more often than not, that left you with nowhere to go.

High school was a blur of running down the loose girls from the bigger towns and courting the special girl at home. Dick played some sports in high school, mainly baseball and basketball. The high school had no football team. Dick and his friends did little drinking and when the few got out of hand, Dick played the role of enforcer, knocking some sense into his delinquent friends. Dick Wallrath met his first wife, Betty, in high school. Betty was a beautiful young woman. They dated for nearly a year, before Betty moved to a larger town, but she continued to run with Dick Wallrath. Dick and Betty married just after high school graduation in 1948, much to the chagrin of four parents, bound together by the poverty they all endured and now the union they so grudgingly accepted.The teenage marriage, a baby during the first year and a move to Houston did not mix well with Dick's unemployment and the suffocating lack of money

Job searches finally found a labor foreman's position and a cheap apartment in a very seedy Houston neighborhood. College was out of the question. Dick Wallrath had a baby and a wife to support. He needed to learn how to become a carpenter and provide for that family. He needed to be gone seven days a week to provide for that family. He needed to extend himself to find any means necessary to support his family. The solution he found was alcohol. The remarkable sense of right and wrong was soon to leave Dick Wallrath for many years.

Alcohol brought Dick back to the life of a child. Dick never was without work after settling in Houston. The paychecks rolled in consistently even under the dome of constant alcohol consumption. Betty didn't drink and doled out the dollars after Dick brought home his paycheck. She had to give him ten or twenty dollars to drink with or he would go and blow the entire paycheck on alcohol. Betty saw the wisdom in treating her husband like a child with an allowance rather than demanding he give up the drinking entirely. Dick and Betty Wallrath had five children during their tumultuous marriage. Michael was the oldest. Michael was born in Houston in 1949. Daniel was born two years later. Joni was born two after Danny and Pamela was born two years after Joni. Dina (Deede), the youngest, was born thirteen years after Michael was born.

Michael lives in Centerville, Texas. Michael has four children, Telina, Mark, Brandy and Shelley. Shelley passed away some years ago at age fourteen. Michael remembers a good relationship with his mother and still maintains that good relationship today. Betty lives in Sattler, Texas. Sattler is wedged between San Marcos and New Braunfels near the Guadalupe River. Betty was a strict mother, but not nearly as strict as Dick had become. The first house the family had was without plumbing and employed a coal burning stove for heat. Michael's job at five years old was to grab his wagon and fetch the coal for the stove. Michael and Danny would get their baths in a washtub set up in the middle of the living room floor.

Michael remembered that his father was a carpenter. Dick would take the boys to work and have them act as his helpers. They weren't much use, but the early memories were carved into Michael's mind. Dick was strict and the boys were afraid of him. No was no and there wasn't any talking back or negotiations on parental orders. Dick Wallrath was an extension of his own father and values were instilled at the end of a leather belt.

Michael Wallrath: I distinctly remember the "bone crusher". Dad would fetch his razor belt. Sometimes we needed it, but other times I felt like we were gettin' whupped just cause it was Tuesday. We were afraid of Dad. He was an alcoholic, but we didn't know nothin' about that back then.

Betty Wallrath walked on eggshells during those early years. In Galena Park, Michael recalled the constant fighting between his parents. Dick would come home and insisted on a special meal like a steak when the rest of the family had a much simpler meal. If the meal was not prepared to his liking, Dick would throw it on the floor. Alcohol precipitated every disagreement. The years took their toll on the children. They knew something wasn't right, but it wasn't until Michael reached the age of twelve that his uncle explained the problems caused by Dick's drinking.

Pamela Wallrath was born in 1955. Pam lives in Arlington, Texas and is married to Bruce, an American Jet International pilot. Bruce is Pam's second husband and they have been married for five years. Pam was married in 1975 and had two children from that first marriage, Garrett and Justin. Pam is a teaching assistant, a full time working teacher without a four-year degree. Pam has been teaching for fifteen years. Pam's early memories of growing up began with a small two-bedroom house in Galena, Texas. The first bedroom was for Dick and Betty. The second bedroom was for the five children. Dick had built a semi-partition in the second bedroom. On one side Danny and Michael slept. On the other side, Joni and Pam shared a double bed along side Deede's crib.

Pam Wallrath Dolenz: I don't have that many memories of my Dad because he was never around. Dad used to keep a flask of whiskey under the front seat of the car. One day, Danny and Michael found the flask and thought it would be funny to empty it out and fill it with Kool-Aid. Dad failed to find the humor in that stunt and the razor belt got some workout that night. I thought he was going to whup those boys all night.

Betty Wallrath had her hands full. She balanced two jobs most of the time. Betty worked at the gas company and the thrift shop in town. The thrift shop job helped when they needed clothes for the kids. Vacations consisted of piling the five kids into the car and driving back to Indiana to visit relatives. Dick never accompanied the family on those trips.

Pam Wallrath Dolenz: I began to realize the problem that alcohol was causing somewhere around my junior high years. I would try to stay at my friend's houses as much as possible. Mom had to finally make me come home. We all tried to avoid Dad when he was drunk. In high school, I began to see how other families interacted. I watched other fathers interact with their daughters. Alcohol robbed me of a childhood and a Dad. It makes me so mad, now. I see the good in Dad and that was there back then, but something had a lock on all the good things in his heart and by the time Dad figured it out, we were all grown.

Baseball was the sport of choice for Michael Wallrath. In Galena Park, Michael was excited because this would be the first time he got to wear a baseball uniform. The other leagues he had been a part of were less organized. The kids just wore t-shirts to identify the teams. At twelve years old, Michael was a good pitcher. Dick would show up at some of the games, but his drinking made those appearances less than memorable.

Michael Wallrath: I can recall the year I started to play ball in Galena Park. I had pitched seven or eight games that year and we won them all. On this particular night, I had given up only two hits and we were coasting to a victory. Dad showed up and started yelling at me. He yanked me out of the game because I walked a batter. He made me so nervous that I could never find the strike zone. It was hard back then. Dad had a problem and I was just too young to know it. I remember hoping that he wouldn't make it to my games.

Dick was just as hard on Danny. Both boys would say that their father was just one strict, mean sonofabitch. Regardless of his demeanor, the boys kept seeking Dick's approval. Most boys never grow out of that state. Michael recalled learning to drive while chauffeuring his father to and from the beer joints. Michael began the taxi service at age twelve. Michael would sit in the bar with his father and drive him home when the money ran out or the bar closed.

There were fishing and hunting trips. Dick would take Michael and Danny down to the coast near Galveston to fish. The Wallrath boys and their father would always end up at the west-end of Galveston to do some wade fishing. There was a large undertow and the water could be very dangerous, but Dick went after those speckled trout and red fish with the necessary fishing gear and a fifth of whiskey. Dick would get drunk and run the boats into the oyster reefs. The trips always ended with Dick knee-walking in the surf and along the shore, yelling at the boys and looking for another pop. It was always a mess.

Michael Wallrath: I remember one hunting trip to Normangee. Dad made some barroom deal to lease the hunting rights to a property just outside of Normangee. There was a cabin on the property and when we got, there was already someone in the cabin. Dad had me and

Danny target the vehicle next to the cabin. We let the air out of the tires. Dad busted into

that cabin with a loaded shotgun like John Wayne. It was a miracle that no one was shot.

Turns out, that the property was involved in a bitter divorce. The woman owned the prop-

erty rights and the man Dad made the hunting deal with had no right to lease the land. It

was another bar deal gone bad. We had to take the tires off that car, carry them back to

town, fill 'em up and bring 'em back to the cabin. Man, I just couldn't wait to get married

and get gone!"

There were two distinct personality trends in the Wallrath family. Michael, Pamela and

Deede were so much alike. They had a non-confrontational approach to their lives. Pam,

Michael and Deede took after their mother from day one. Joni and Danny took a page from

their father. They were high strung, stubborn, welled up with pride and resentment. Danny

and Joni were driven with much the same focus as their father. Michael and Pam agreed

that the same headstrong pride in Dick, Danny and Joni has kept the three stubborn mules

at arm's length.

Michael Wallrath: The best moment I can remember with my father was when he called

Danny and me into his office at Champion Windows. In a military style, Dad told us how

much he loved us. I was twenty-four years old and Danny was twenty-two. The bottle took

away many things from us as children, but the one constant issue to remember is so impor-

tant to keep a hold of. That bottle could have taken so much more.

Strength is a genetic level of evolution. Never has an example of perseverance and tenacity defined adulthood better than in the lives of Dick Wallrath's children. Whether acceptance was in the form of example or malevolence, the results were undeniable. Michael, Danny, Joni, Pam and Deede have exhibited remarkable strength when they could have easily packed it in and snuggled up inside a cocoon of outside blame.

Pam Wallrath Dolenz: Dad came to grips with his addiction by channeling the addictive forces within his body to success. When Dad came to terms with the damage caused by his drinking, he became that much more determined to pull his life above the level to which he had fallen.

The Wallrath children and Betty had to wait and watch for a man to emerge. God gave everyone the strength to achieve his or her just goals, but did not dictate the timetable by which to arrive. Dick Wallrath's path eventually led to a separate journey, but his children and their mother never wavered from the desire to be better parents and better spouses. As they all well knew, success within those roles was not a birthright, success was the result of loving from a place that only they shared together.

Pam Wallrath Dolenz: None of us can go back and change what has already occurred. Anger proved to accomplish very little. When I had trouble in my first marriage, I found strength from my younger sister, Deede, who was very ill at the time. My first husband was a replica of my father in many ways. He was focused, determined to achieve success and domineering. Deede gave me the path to walk on my own and eventually find the man I now adore. I've never been certain why some women are attracted to the men they choose, but I have always loved my father. I have been angry at him, but through his faults and weaknesses, I have become a better woman and a better parent. Through his strengths and accomplishments, I have become a better woman and a better parent. I can remember when my father forced me to eat an oyster after returning from a fishing expedition. I was pretty young and wanted nothing to do with those little buggers. I gagged. I couldn't stand to look at that oyster and I certainly couldn't stand the taste. Dad felt pretty bad when I cried about eating that oyster. Now, I can't get enough of those slimy little delicacies. I love them to death. I wonder if that wasn't just a bit providential?

CHAPTER 2

Chapter Two…Scholarship #1, Kayla Rathman

"To the world you may be one person, but to that one person you may be the world"…that is how I sum up Dick Wallrath. I am humbled today to be chosen as one of the few to write about Mr. Wallrath and what he means to me. We have a very special relationship, one I cherish every day.

It was the summer of 2000. I was in College Station, Texas to receive an Opportunity Scholarship from the Texas 4-H Foundation. When you arrive for the assembly, you have no idea how big your scholarship will be or who will sponsor it. Scholarships range from $1500 up to $10,000. I was very fortunate to receive a $10,000 scholarship from the Houston Livestock Show and Rodeo sponsored by Mr. Dick Wallrath. I returned home from Roundup and wrote my scholarship donor a Thank You letter. Weeks later, I received a letter back from Mr. Wallrath. This was a first! I had written many Thank You letters in my eighteen years and never received correspondence. So I placed the card in a safe place and the day I left for college, I took the card with me. As many of you know the first semester of college is…very hectic and you just try to keep your head above water…so needless to say, I never did anything with that card that semester. I just tucked it away safely in a drawer.

During Christmas break of that year, something happened that made me pick up that card and do something with it. My family and I lost my grandparents in a tragic car accident. I had a hole in my heart and carried much sadness as many of you have too when you have lost someone close to you. Kobi Yamada once said "Believe that there's light at the end of the tunnel. Believe that you may be that light for someone else." My light was in that little card that held hope inside of it. Days before I was to intern in the AgVenture area of the Houston Livestock Show and Rodeo, I called my scholarship donor. He agreed to meet

with me in Houston during the show. On Valentine's Day of 2001, which also would have

been my Mimi's birthday, I met a very special man. I will never forget that day. When he

came walking into the swine area, I knew it had to be him. For those of you who know

Dick Wallrath, chances were better than average that he would not be touring the area with

a sow and her piglets for the heck of it. He was there for one reason and that reason was

me. Mr. Wallrath has the heart of an angel and the tenacity of a lion. You all know the

importance of the work he has done, but no one understands that better than me. It is

because of him that I have two degrees from Texas A&M University. He allowed me to

achieve my goals and dreams. Thank you just doesn't seem to be enough. Since the ini-

tial meeting in Houston, I have had several opportunities to visit the ranch. I was four

hours away from home during college so it made it very nice to be able to drive an hour

and visit with Patsy and Mr. Wallrath at the ranch. Patsy has fixed several meals for me.

She is a great cook! I am indebted to her as well. I try to visit at least once every couple

of months.

In 2003, I completed my Bachelor of Science degree in three years graduating Magna Cum

Laude. Mr. Wallrath was there the day I walked the stage at Texas A&M. I chose to further my

education and pursue a Master's degree with the funds from my HLSR scholarship. In 2004, I

wrapped up my college experience and accepted a position with the Texas 4-H Foundation as

the Director of the Texas 4-H Friends and Alumni Association.

It is hard to put into words how grateful I am for Mr. Wallrath. He came into my life at

the perfect time and he has always been very encouraging and supportive. I see him as my

grandfather. I keep him up-to-date with what is going on in my life and where I am headed next. He treats me like family and tells me like it is. There is no sugar coating any-

thing. I always hear his words in the back of my mind "You got to have goals, you have

to know where you are going in life". I got that speech the second time I met him.

Mr. Wallrath has impacted me in a way few people ever will and all I can do is make sure

that he knows how much I appreciate him. "Some people come into your life and quickly

go, but others leave footprints on your heart and you are never the same." Mr. Wallrath,

Thank You from the bottom of my heart!

Kayla Kohls Rathmann

2000 4-H Scholarship Recipient

CHAPTER 3

Chapter Three...A Power Greater than the Vice-President

Guilt is a powerful fuel that rejuvenates at the drop of a hat. Dick Wallrath was filled with guilt for most of his waking moments. The solution to that guilt was to drink more. Alcohol was the prize for feeling bad, for feeling good, for feeling sad or for feeling energized. As the years rolled on into a series of memory losses and missed birthday parties, Dick began to wonder what was wrong with him. Guilt produced the sense that he was wrong on everything he did in his life. For the most part, he was.

Dick Wallrath: I wasn't there for my wife. I wasn't there for my kids. I questioned everything I did in my life except the alcohol. I couldn't figure out what was wrong, so I drank some more to help me figure it out. My daddy told me, that even a busted clock is right two times a day.

The flavor of the day was beer and straight whiskey. Dick kept a pint under the front seat of the car at all times. During most of his drinking years, he could get through the day and function at work without drinking. In the latter stages of his drinking, the whiskey found a home in his belly during the day as well. Dick normally picked the bars that were far away from his home, but not too far because he had to navigate the way home while thoroughly drunk. The long distance from home made it more difficult for his wife to locate him and find out exactly what was going on at those bars.

Dick Wallrath: I was living in Galena Park with a wife and five kids. The date was somewhere around 1965 and I was a drunk. I had a dream one night and I remember the dream so vividly because it was in color, bright vibrant colors. Everything good in my life had turned to crap due to alcohol. I had become a liar and a thief. If I could skin you out of $200, then by God I had that money before you could blink. I would make claims on a construction site about work that had already been done when, in fact, the work had never been started, much less completed. By the time I had to explain the problem, I was drunk. Everything was for me. The dream made me take a long hard look at myself and I was repulsed. I thought about suicide, but I didn't have the guts.

Alcoholism wasn't discussed much back in those days. Today, it seems like every family has an alcoholic or a drug addict and the family joins together to help the abuser face their issues. There are interventions, qualified social workers, educated psychologists, and terrific treatment programs available throughout the country. The legal option for many first and second time criminals is treatment versus jail. In 1965, the family had few options. They simply did not invite Uncle Bob to the family picnics or to Thanksgiving dinner. Everyone knew Uncle Bob would get drunk and ruin the evening. The fear of addiction or dependency has traveled a great distance in the public eye, as well. On July 31, 1972, Senator Thomas Eagleton announced his intention to withdraw as the Democratic running mate to George McGovern. Eagleton had been hospitalized three times for exhaustion and twice received electric shock therapy. R. Sargent Shriver replaced Eagleton as the Democratic Vice Presidential candidate. McGovern/Shriver lost in a huge landslide to Nixon/Agnew. Five years ago, then presidential candidate George Bush stood before the nation and said, hell yes, I had a problem and I don't have one now.

Dick Wallrath was running out of time. The alcohol was not only taking the toll on the family, but it was controlling his life. Dick and his construction crew used to frequent a local establishment near his Galena Park residence. On one occasion, the young attractive waitress had mentioned to Dick and the boys that one of the African-American (not the term offered up in the day) cooks had gotten drunk the night before and had taken up residence in her car. She mentioned that she was leaving soon and could not get the man out of the car. Dick offered to remove the slightly inebriated employee from her car. Dick pulled the man from the car. He was sleeping it off and did not wake up when the car door was pulled open. The man woke up quickly when his head bounced off the parking lot asphalt. The young man jumped up and went after Dick, who had a few pops under his belt already. Dick cold-cocked the charging cook and dropped him quickly. Dick took to working on that man with his boots and had to be pulled away by some of his crew. They rolled the man under a nearby trailer, as they were near a trailer park. When Dick sobered up, he got scared to death, certain that he had killed a man on the previous day. Dick watched the local papers for days and finally reached a logical solution when it became apparent that the man had not died. Dick decided that he would avoid fights when he was drunk because his temper had the capability to get him in some serious trouble.

Dick Wallrath: I put the hustle on my best friend's wife. I won't mention his name, but he was my dearest friend in the world. One day, when I knew he wasn't home and I had consumed the better part of a quart of whiskey, I had the insatiable idea to visit my friend's wife and she would be unable to control her desire to be with me. She was quite able to control her desire to be with me and exhibited a desire to get away from me. She told her husband about my visit and I ruined a terrific friendship because I was drunk and didn't think. That could be the description of each day of my life for those years. I didn't think.

Dick's sister in Galena Park knew a very successful plumber that had been living the twelve-step program for a number of years. He was anxious to meet with Dick Wallrath. Dick had come to the realization that something was terribly wrong and he didn't know how to fix it. Dick decided that he didn't want to live any longer if he couldn't change his life around. That was the decision to make his first visit to learn about living his life without alcohol.

The Chief of Police in Galena Park was a friend of the family. He knew Dick and liked him, but he knew there was something Dick had to address. Dick would call the Police Chief on occasion and ask to be allowed to stay in jail for a few days to dry out. The Chief told Dick that drying out in jail for a few days would not fix anything. He allowed it, but talked at length about Dick's need to find a more permanent solution. The Chief accompanied Dick to his first few meetings. Dick was sobered up fast with the thought of baring his soul at a meeting. Dick was appalled with the sight of much older men and women wallowing in self-pity and incapable of something so simple as handling a few drinks. Dick Wallrath's first foray into the world of acknowledging alcohol addiction did not lead to immediate success. The first step, however, would eventually change his life completely.

Dick Wallrath: The first couple of meetings were helpful. I listened to people who seemed to have the same issues that I was dealing with. Sobriety lasted nearly ninety days the first time I tried it. Then, I decided that somehow I was smarter and better equipped to cope with alcohol than any of them were. Shit, I could quit drinking anytime I wanted to. Hell, I had quit drinking seven times alone last week. Those people at the meetings looked too old to drink, but I was still pretty young and they couldn't handle it. I could.

The nights didn't get better. It had been more than two years since Dick Wallrath had been to his first twelve-step meeting. He had quit drinking for two straight years, every other week. Dick pulled a knife on a guy in barroom dispute and came close to using it before the argument found another solution. Time was not on Dick's side. Life was a catastrophe and the self-induced spiral would not stop unless Dick pulled himself out of the free-fall or until the free-fall killed him.

Dick Wallrath: I had finally had enough. It was not one specific incident that sent me back for good. I was working as a framing carpenter and I felt like I had tremendous drive to locate success. I worked on Saturdays and Sundays. Guilt consumed me when I sat down to rest. I discovered alcohol and this drug allowed me to remain in my fantasy world. Alcohol was my God in a bottle and after nearly eighteen years of abuse, I ended up unemployable, with five children and hopelessly careening to a catastrophe for me, my family or anyone close to me. I had gone to a Chamber of Commerce meeting with my wife in Pasadena, Texas. We listened to a speaker by the name of Robert Gilmour LeTourneau from Longview, Texas. I was half drunk, but something got through the haze. A number of contractors had a construction deal to build a major dam in the desert near Las Vegas. The last drop of concrete was poured into that dam in May, 1935. In 1947, the dam was named after the man so instrumental in pursuing the project. The Hoover Dam was born. Some of the contractors contacted Mr. LeToruneau about the issues related to such a large project and the primitive methods available to complete the dam. Mr. LeTourneau invented many of the earth moving machines used in the actual construction of the dam. Many of those machines are still used today in road construction. Mr. Robert Gilmour LeTourneau designed his earthmoving equipment as early as 1922. Credited with inventing the first modern scraper, Mr. LeTourneau's next invention was called the "Mountain Mover." This earthmoving marvel could carry twelve cubic yards of gravel or dirt, unheard of in those days. LeTourneau's machines kept getting bigger and better with load capacities reaching twenty-four, thirty, forty-two and finally sixty cubic yards. In 1953, Mr. LeTourneau sold the business to Westinghouse Air Co. The original LeTourneau designs and patents have been broadened and refined ever since.

Mr. Letourneau spoke for nearly thirty minutes. When he started his business, he pledged to give twenty percent of his profits to God and keep eighty percent. When the business sputtered and grew slowly, he reversed the percentages. Mr. Letourneau pledged to give eighty percent of his earnings to God and to keep twenty percent. His business exploded. His statement: "when giving to charity and when given from the heart, there is no way you can out give God," I thought that was the craziest thing I had ever heard. A few nights later, I had my dream, about the person I had become. Like I said earlier, it was not a specific incident that triggered action, but a series of poor decisions over nearly two decades. It was one specific life that had sped out of control. I listened to the words I had heard so many times before. "We abandon ourselves to God as we know God. We clear away the wreckage of our past and give freely of what we find." This was my miracle.

In the text revered by those stricken by the disease of alcoholism, the simplicity of the program is remarkable. The difficulty to live within the program is staggering. "Rarely has a person failed who has thoroughly followed our path. Those who do not recover are people who cannot or will not completely give themselves to the program, usually men and women who are constitutionally incapable of being honest with themselves."*

Dick Wallrath stumbled through those first months and years of sobriety and the attempt to live without alcohol. The chances of successfully extraditing alcohol from the lifestyle to which an individual had grown accustomed to were razor thin. Weakness to defeat alcohol is not a personal flaw or developmental defect in character. The inability to exorcise the demons of alcohol is a genetic parody. While accepting alcohol as a religion inside a bottle, many take to heart that the answers lie within the problem. The disease of alcohol becomes the solution to the problems it creates. The enormity of sobriety is endless, yet so simple. Success rises like the sun on a steamy Texas summer day, when each day is the only day to worry about. The alcoholic cannot get drunk today if he does not take a drink today. The alcoholic must not concern himself with tomorrow.

Dick Wallrath: The ability to recover from the disease of alcohol has come about by the grace of a very loving God. I am not and have never been a bible thumper. I was told in the twelve-step program that I had to muster up a higher power of my own. I was raised in a Baptist church and taught about Jesus. For some reason, every time that I prayed to Jesus, I felt like I was going to the Vice-President and I was somehow not good enough to speak to the man himself. To me, God is not a person. God is nature, the sun and the moon. God is love and the good within us all. The image of God has never spoken to me, but I hear him and see him every day in all of us. I give God the credit in my life for all the good things and I take credit for all the screw-ups.

I have learned through the twelve-step program about who I am and who I wanted to become. I became aware of the seven negative emotions and the seven positive emotions. What are these emotions and what place do they have in my life? There are two kinds of fear, real and imaginary. We need the real fear so we do not stand in front of a freight train or an oncoming truck. The imaginary fear is what defeats us. Hate is self-explanatory. Resentment is a relived moment of anger against a person, place or situation. Jealousy is the insanity of change. Greed, lust and envy can all form the foundations of addiction and most certainly add fuel to the engine while it is running. On the positive side you have faith, hope, desire, enthusiasm, love, sex and romance. I am grateful for my faith in God and work hard to always maintain true faith in myself. I retain hope for the future and try to live my life in accordance with what I have done and what I have yet to do. I have a desire to reach and achieve goals. I have enthusiasm to go forth in a positive manner. I will always continue to learn about the meaning of love. I want my children and my family and my friends to have patience with me and grow with me as I discover how to give of myself each and every day. Sex is God given and romance will never die.

Success is not just an affirmation of intent. Success in every phase of life is not a wishing game or a whining alternative to failure. Success is a state of mind and a state of effort. The two must go hand in hand. Dick Wallrath had the guts of a burglar and the courage to live his life without alcohol, when the subject of alcoholism was barely addressed. Celebrities didn't revel in rehab programs. Betty Ford was a congressman's wife with her own drinking and addiction issues. In July, 1960 a book was published that spoke to define Dick Wallrath's epiphany and his mantra to succeed in business and life. The book, *Think and Grow Rich by Napoleon Hill*, had been the basis for the Dale Carnegie sales course and seminars. Andrew Carnegie commissioned Mr. Hill to write a book on what it took to be successful. The foundations of Mr. Hill's book and the struggling simplicity of the twelve-step program pulled Dick Wallrath from the race he had been losing to the path of self-direction. Once Mr. Wallrath figured out what he was willing to give up in order to achieve his goals, then the climb to achieve those goals became a forgone conclusion.

Foremost in Dick Wallrath's rise to success was the acceptance of the twelve-step program born in July 1935. It was Akron, Ohio and a prominent physician was spiraling out of control. The Eighteenth Amendment had been passed and society as a whole was given the green light to consume all the alcohol they could get their hands on. When that prominent Ohio physician met Bill W., "the first living human being with whom I had ever talked, who knew what he was talking about in regard to alcoholism from actual experience" *, the foundations for recovery were born.

*"If you think you are an atheist, an agnostic, a skeptic, or have any other form of intellectual pride which keeps you from accepting what is in this book, I feel sorry for you. If you think you are strong enough to beat the game alone, that is your affair. But if you really want to quit drinking liquor for good and all, and sincerely feel that you must have some help, we know that we have an answer for you. It never fails, if you go about it with one-half the zeal you have been in the habit of showing when you were getting another drink."***

The twelve-step program has a personal meaning to everyone that has ever embraced the teachings. Dick Wallrath had the courage to read much more than the words on the page. Talk is a good game when recovering. The day the talk is abandoned and the message is felt in the heart is the day recovery will begin. How did the twelve steps relate to Dick Wallrath?

1) We admitted we were powerless over alcohol and that our lives had become unmanageable.

Dick Wallrath: I was at that point before I got to any meetings. I really didn't know what was wrong with me. I had many thoughts that I was losing my mind when I tried to explain the stunts I had been pulling in my life while drunk. I was almost relieved when I discovered through my meetings that I was afflicted with the disease of alcoholism. I was thirty-eight years old and I was not prone to readily admit anything could whup my ass. Well, alcohol had whupped it good. My sister, Jo White made me promise to go see a plumber in Galena Park named Bob Sawyer. Bob was a recovered alcoholic. He took me to my first meeting and the gosh darn thing made sense. I went to a meeting every day for the first ninety days, then I figured I got smart. These people were too old too drink and I could quit any time. I started drinking again and sped in and out of an alcohol induced fog for another three years. The last half of that third year, I wanted to get sober more than anything in the world and I drank every day. I finally went back to the meetings I had begun three years before. I saw something in the faces and the eyes of those attending the meetings. They were happy. Whatever it took to find what they had, I was now willing to do. I drank two pints of whiskey and a case of beer per day. I woke up and felt like shit, but I'd do it all over again. I'd grab for Earl around the toilet and wake up the next morning ready for another round. My life had to change and I never wanted anything more. I always had a belief in God, but I was about to find out why.

2) Came to believe that a Power greater than ourselves could restore us to sanity.

Dick Wallrath: I was raised in the church and always believed in God. I asked God to get me out of many bad situations and if he did, then I was going to straighten out my life, but I never did. When I went back to the meetings for good, I was told to find a God that I could understand. I finally came up with an image of god that worked for me and that I could understand. God is nature, as I have said before. He is the goodness I see in every human being and therefore I do not have to search for God at all. He is in every person I see. He is around me every day and every moment of weakness and strength.

3) Made a decision to turn our will and our lives over to the care of God as we understand God.

Dick Wallrath: I had a very difficult time locating an image of God that I could understand and relate to. The conception of God baffled me. Take the old preacher at the filling station. He is packed up with all his belongings, his family and his pulpit. Asked what his mission is, the preacher replied that he was told by God to go down to Galveston and open another church. Well, it turns out that he was fired in East Texas for screwing the piano player. I had an awful time wrapping my head around the way people made a mockery of God's will and my search for something that I could understand. I knew that twisting and turning of "God's will" would not work for me. A good friend put it best after I had near-

ly given up searching for something I could call a Power greater than ourselves. My friend

simply told me, that the only difference between us and the other animals on this planet is

that God gave us the ability to know right from wrong. When you did right, you felt good.

When you did something wrong, you felt ill.

We could feel it inside our hearts. It didn't take a preacher or a counselor to tell us that.

Therefore, the good I saw in each person was the image of God giving us the option. The

conventional rhetoric of religion revolves around eternity. Do you know what eternity is?

I don't. Eternity to me is, waking up at three in the morning and wanting a drink. The liquor

store doesn't open until ten o'clock. That is eternity. My sponsor told me that I had to get

me a God that I could understand because I was libel to get his drunk. He also told me that

when I found my God, that I didn't have to follow him for the rest of my life. I had to fol-

low him one day at a time. I didn't have to quit drinking for the rest of my life, I had to

quit drinking for today. If I didn't have a drink today, then I couldn't get drunk today. As

soon as I grasped the concept of one day at a time, the boat quit rockin'.

4) Made a searching and fearless moral inventory of ourselves.

Dick Wallrath: Any business that doesn't take an inventory is likely to go broke. People

have to do the same thing. Sometimes we can go it alone and sometimes we need the help

of friends and family. My sponsor was an ex-school teacher named Dave Prayther. Dave

was a humble man and very wise. He taught me to take an inventory of myself like a busi-

ness. Put down the good points and the bad points of your own personality. This is where the story about the broken clock came to mind. Even a broken clock is right twice a day. Look at the bad points and work on them. You may need to work on your ego or your temper. The list, if honest, would dictate the weaknesses. Our weaknesses are like cancers. If we ignore them , they grow and eventually eat us alive.

5) Admitted to God, to ourselves and to another human being the exact nature of our wrongs.

Dick Wallrath: That is what we do from the taking stock in our moral inventory. The interesting thing that I clearly remember about those early lists is that I did have some good traits. Hell, I had a boatload of work to do on my temper, my resentment issues, my ego, my drinking certainly, you name it, but I was relieved to find out that I was not a black hole of evil.

6) Were entirely ready to have God remove all these defects of character.

Dick Wallrath: Everything associated with the twelve-step program is about willingness and the desire to change. Step Six is about crossing the line forever. Catholics confess their sins to a priest and then go about their lives. Alcoholics confess theirs sins and weaknesses to their own image of God and then prepare for the removal of those defects. There are those of us who simply cannot accept the simple truths to life. A man asked me recently, how wishing God would remove your shortcomings could actually accomplish the task? I was reminded that wishing and hoping for things did not make them come true. Napolean Hill's book on success is adamant about the effort coupled with desire achieves success.

The effort in the twelve-step program is in finding a God that you can understand and trusting that image to help you accomplish anything. My answer to that man, who could not envision asking God to accomplish what he had not been able to accomplish, was to ask him if he ever tried it?

7) Humbly ask God to remove our shortcomings.

Dick Wallrath: This relates to what I talked about in Step Six. It also relates to Step Three, but now we turn our attention to the specifics. We now begin to take actions to assure the success of our convictions. For example, if a man drives across the lane in front of me and cuts me off hard, my first reaction may be to honk, flash a middle finger salute and hope he pulls over so we can duke it out. He may have been in a hurry for a reason that I cannot conceive of. His daughter may have been hurt at school or he may have been a firefighter racing to a station without the benefit of a flashing light. We work on stepping back to accept the good in everyone instead of assuming the worst and accepting violence as a good solution to the confrontation.

8) Made a list of all persons we had harmed, and became willing to make amends to them all.

Dick Wallrath: Here is the time to make a list of all those harmed during your drinking days. We will make a concentrated effort to repair the damage done during those years except when the effort may cause further damage to themselves or others. If I had an affair with a neighbor, I wouldn't go to the neighbor and apologize for my indiscretion.

The apology would hurt someone else. If someone does not accept the attempt to rectify a past wrong, then you have done what you could do. I had owed some money to an older man for more than a decade. He did some work on my cars and I never paid him for it. When I went to see the man, he was in the hospital. He was quite old. I had a beard and he had not seen me in ten or fifteen years. I hadn't got to within two-hundred feet of the room and he called my name. He was tickled to see me. That floored me. His name was Carl Elmore. I told him that I was there to make restitution for an old debt. I asked him how much did I owe him? He didn't have a clue. He told me that his filling station had burned down and he lost all his records and he didn't really care now. I gave Carl what I thought I owed him plus interest. My family was on my list, but dredging up many of my short-comings as a father when I was drinking, put them back into an arena that surrounded only pain. In hindsight, I should have included my children and my wife to a greater degree in this step. All they had known was my drinking. When I saw the reaction to my sobriety, then I was reluctant to immerse my children back into what I had done. I was reluctant to relive my infidelity and offend Betty again. Looking back, that may have been an easier way out for me. Some wounds may have healed quicker and some existing wounds may have been addressed better. We all make mistakes and being sober doesn't mean our mis-takes will vanish. All we can do is acknowledge the mistakes and make every effort not to repeat them.

9) Made direct amends to such people whenever possible, except when to do so would injure them or others.

Dick Wallrath: This is the action phase of Step Eight. We have made a list of people to visit and Step Nine is the action of consequence. Step Nine is the bridge to accepting the past as something that you cannot change. There are so many things in an alcoholic's life that he or she would change if given the opportunity. That will not happen and never has. We cannot change the past. We can only make certain that we live as better individuals. We can only begin to live the kind of life that God meant us to lead.

10) Continued to take personal inventory and when we were wrong promptly admitted it.

Dick Wallrath: That is the daily maintenance. We're not Saints. We don't walk on water. I haven't grown any halos, lately. I still lose my temper now and then. I am still a human being and I need to monitor my progress, every day. If I do something wrong, I try to rectify that by the end of the day. I can recall many meetings with bankers where I had lost my temper. They sit up above you like schoolteachers and look down at you while you pitch the reasons for the business loan you may be seeking. I have sent many apology notes for my behavior at certain banks. It is part of the process. I still need a good swift shot to the chin on occasion to knock me in line.

11) Sought through prayer and meditation to improve our conscious contact with God as we understand God, for us and the power to carry that out.

Dick Wallrath: Believe me, I could screw up a two-car funeral. A dry drunk is an alcoholic that has gone over the edge but simply has not reached for the bottle yet. It is only a matter of time. This is where our convictions and our spiritual relationships have to be maintained. There are no shortcuts and there are no angles to weasel your way around staying in touch with a Power greater than us. Drinking isn't a marathon where the runner hits the wall and takes a rest. After ten years of sobriety, we cannot reflect back and think that now we can have a few beers or a glass of wine with dinner. Our lives are better, work is better, now we could re-introduce alcohol into our lives. That cannot happen in my life. If I am thinking that, then I am losing contact with God and the strength that got me to quit in the first place. I remember going to Germany on a vacation. I was staying at a very nice hotel in Frankfurt. There was a river-walk similar to the river-walk in San Antonio near the hotel. I would go down there and get my exercise for the day. It was a great place to run. I was in the middle of a run when I noticed a man on a public bench. I stopped and stared for a moment. The man was dressed in a very expensive suit, maybe a thousand dollars or more. He had a set of equally expensive luggage with him. He was passed out on the bench. He had vomited on himself and had pissed in his pants. If I ever loose my way with God, that man could easily be me. God put him there for me to see what would happen if I decided to take another drink. The only thing I had to give up was my right to drink today. That has worked for thirty-seven years.

12) Having had a spiritual awakening as the result of these steps, we tried to carry this message to alcoholics, and to practice these principles in all our affairs.

Dick Wallrath: I look at this gift like a big note from the bank. I can never really repay the principle on my loan. God carries that. All I can do is make some small interest payments back on the principle. Each time I work with a drunk, sponsor a drunk, or make a speech at a meeting is a small payment on the interest. I will never lose the ability to identify with anyone afflicted with the disease of alcoholism. I want everyone to know that from whence I came, so can you. The twelve-step program gave me life. It's not a whole lot to ask for me to pass that on whenever I can.

*, **...The Fourth Edition of the Big Book.

CHAPTER 4

Chapter Four...Kara A. Van Maren

"In Memory of Dina Wallrath Robertson by Champion Windows."   I want to take this opportunity to thank Mr. Wallrath for the 2004 Houston Livestock Show and Rodeo Scholarship in the amount of $10,000. I was honored to be a recipient. I would also like to thank Mr. Wallrath on behalf of all the teens involved in the various programs for his continued support in both the agricultural area and the academic area. With Mr. Wallrath's support and encouragement, teens are able to achieve their dreams.

Many people believe that living in a small town doesn't present as many opportunities as larger cities present. I say they are wrong. I believe that people have to make their own opportunities. I moved to Riviera, Texas at the beginning of second grade. I had been there many times before to see my grandparents. We often stayed throughout the summers. I always enjoyed running through the cornfields, swimming in the lake and playing in the pastures. My cousins and I absolutely loved finding old cow bones, dragging them back up to the main house and reconstructing the whole cow in my grandmother's yard. Needless to say, my grandmother was less than thrilled by our excavation projects. My grandfather always took us out to help pick the cotton, drive the tractor and feed all the horses and cows. We'd all load up in the back of his truck and have a contest to see who could throw the range cubes the farthest. I loved every minute of being on my grandparent's farm. I was thrilled when my parents told us we were moving to Riviera.

In the third grade, my mom asked me if I wanted to join 4-H. With a hesitant yes, that was it. The door was opened. I remember the day of registration as the day I signed my life away. Turns out, it was the day that opened more doors than anyone could have imagined. My first year, I signed up to exhibit a swine project and a horse project. I remember how

61

excited I was when we pulled into the drive of Seimnesma Hog Farm to pick out my very first pig. As we fell out of the Suburban, the owner told us that we were in for a treat. A sow had just delivered a litter of piglets about an hour earlier. We selected a nice Duroc gilt, loaded her up and took her home. That year I learned the proper nutrition for show swine and the importance of exercise. I had some beginner's luck at the Kleberg-Kennedy junior Livestock Show that year and sold me pig for one-thousand dollars. The horse project I showed that year was a twenty-two year old quarter horse that my uncle showed in high school. I did it for fun and the experience. The horse competition taught me the rules and techniques to compete in halter, showmanship, western pleasure and horsemanship. My first year in 4-H was a dream come true.

As the years went by, I added and scratched different projects to my registration form. I always raised a swine project. My participation in Consumer Decision Making opened a whole new door for me. My first experience with a major livestock show was when I competed in the Consumer Decision Making Contest at the San Antonio Junior Livestock Show in 1997. In the contest, you evaluate consumer goods and place them according to how they could best serve the needs of the consumer. After many practice sessions and local competitions, the project group from Kleberg County participated in the San Antonio contest. Although I was a sub-junior participant, the junior team needed a fourth and I was moved up. The team placed fourth and I was twelfth in the individual high point. The next two years we continued to place high in all categories.

Over the years, I continued to show Duroc hogs. I learned a great deal from different breeders about market swine. Along with the many successful runs I had, I had to learn how to accept defeat when my pigs didn't make the sale. My swine project expanded from market swine to breeding gilts and from the county shows to major shows. In 2000, after

three years of trying, I finally caught a calf at the Calf Scramble in San Antonio. I decid-

ed to use the certificate to purchase two Duroc gilts and one Spot gilt. Participating in the

breeding shows was a new atmosphere and somewhat overwhelming. It was very demand-

ing to get the gilts ready for the show.

I thoroughly enjoyed the breeding shows, so the next year, I decided to participate in the

Junior Barrow Show at San Antonio. A barrow is a young, castrated male pig. I sold my first San

Antonio Barrow for thirty-eight hundred dollars. I received many awards through 4-H including

Outstanding Sub-Junior, Outstanding Junior and the 4-H Gold Star Award.

I became involved in the leadership and community service activities. I served as

Kleberg-Kennedy 4-H County Council President, 1st Vice-President, 2nd Vice-President

and many other club officer positions. I was also a member of FFA, NHS and Student

Council. These organizations allowed me to develop the people and social skills necessary

to excel in my chosen fields. I have nurtured a love for my community and helping others.

Without 4-H, I'm not certain that I would be this involved. My 4-H career has been a big

part of my life. I spend a great deal of time involved with 4-H activities and helping oth-

ers. Because of 4-H, I would like to become a registered dietician so I can continue to help

young 4-Hers and young people in general to achieve great things in their lives. I am a

sophomore at Texas A & M University. Many of the young people I see on campus are the

same young people that I competed against in the livestock shows around Texas. We all

relive the glory days. The friendships from 4-H and the knowledge that I will always have

those friends that I can call on in times of need, is more comforting than you can imagine.

The ironic aspect to growing up inside 4-H, livestock shows and the overall framework of an agricultural life, is that those people nationally who turn their nose up to anything associated with ranches and farms, know nothing about the tremendous opportunities derived from raising young animals. They know nothing about the strength of character within these organizations. They know nothing about the thousands of kids who are now better parents, better citizens and better neighbors because of 4-H and programs like 4-H. I encourage the youth of tomorrow to live their lives by the 4-H motto, " To Make the Best Better."

I would like to thank Mr. Wallrath again for awarding this scholarship to me. I look forward to corresponding with Mr. Wallrath over the next four years and beyond that. I truly believe that people like Mr. Wallrath inspire others to follow his generous path. As long as these scholarship awards were in the name of his daughter, Mr. Wallrath was content to help them grow each year. Generosity has to be the only true satisfaction from hard work.

Sincerely,

Kara A. Van Maren

CHAPTER 5

Chapter Five...The Window Opened, Champion Windows.

Sobriety did not instantly clear up the financial problems accumulated by the years of drinking and lost focus. While Dick always kept that pint under the front seat of his car or truck, he also made certain that he knew how to build a house from the dry Texas soil to the last drop of paint covering the drywall. The newly sober Texan directed his attention to new employment. The Houston Chronicle job search turned up construction coordinator ads for an annual salary of $10,000. Truck driver positions were offering similar salaries of $10,000. Dick Wallrath had spent the better part of his adult life learning how to build a house the right way. He knew how to work with the inspectors and the contractors. Dick would sell peanuts on the corner before he sold twenty years of construction knowledge for $10,000 per year.

In 1968, Dick answered an ad for Living Window Company in Houston. The job was a window salesman. The sales people had to visit construction sites and sell windows to the builders. Dick was told that he would have to use his own vehicle and the expenses were not covered. The sales people were paid a commission and there would be no salary. Dick reluctantly took the position for reasons unclear back then and to this day, remain somewhat unclear. There is something to be said for arriving in the right place at the right time. Most of our lives are not accidental. We may think we control our lives, but we don't.

Dick was paired up with a man simply called Garnett. Garnett was a big, red-nosed former drunk that lived by the code of raw honesty. Garnett kept a ledger that documented everything that happened on a daily basis. If Dick forgot to do something, there was Garnett, pointing to his ledger and reminding Dick that he said he would do this or do that. The training was invaluable. The only thing Dick Wallrath knew about windows before the

Living Window Company was that they would keep out some of the wind and the water. Windows were a better alternative to a large open hole in a home. That was the extent of the Wallrath window knowledge prior to 1968. Within four years of accepting the position in window sales, Dick Wallrath was close to earning in excess of $100,000 per year.

In the fifth year of his employment at the Living Window Company, Dick had saved nearly $40,000 and made the decision to go into business for himself. A window manufacturer in San Antonio agreed to sell Dick the windows. Dick would start Champion Window Company as a middle man company. They bought and warehoused the windows, then sold the windows to builders in the area. Champion began as a window distributor. Dick went to the owner of Living Window and told him of his new enterprise. Dick assured the man that at no time did he use company time to solicit existing company accounts. Dick mentioned that as soon as he has left the company then he would be all over those accounts like the sap running down a Maple tree. Dick's boss stood up and might have thrown him out of the office. Instead, he wished Dick well and thanked him for being honest about his intentions and honest about soliciting his customers. Dick never believed that honesty was a special virtue that deserved great praise and recognition. Honesty was what a person should do every day. Honesty was like sleep. Everyone needs it, everyone gets some regardless and the more you get, the better you feel.

Dick Wallrath: I knew that the only thing I was ever going to be in that company was a window salesman. I could make some money and save some money, but I had a burning desire to be something more. I wanted to be successful beyond my boundaries and beyond the boundaries that I believed everyone else put around me. I lost so much when I was drinking. I lost the father-son relationships with my boys. I lost the father-daughter relationships with my daughters. I threw out those years because of my alcohol abuse. Deede was young enough that I was able to watch her grow and she was able to get to know me without the drinking. It was beautiful. The closer I got to Deede, the more I knew that the years I lost with my other children were never coming back. There was nothing I could change to get them back. I know that I transferred some of my own guilt into proving something through business and financial success. At least, I could give back in some other ways. I have never been the smartest guy in the world, but I knew that I could not buy back those years. I wanted to put myself and my family in a position where we could chose our paths of reconciliation without financial constraints.

The first year in business on my own was tougher than I could have ever imagined. I knew that I had failed at so many things in my life, that I was so damned determined not to fail at this. I remember going to Acapulco, alone. I stayed at the Princess Hotel. I had not made the decision to start the window company yet. Water was my recluse. I drank up the power of the surf and the calmness within such great strength allowed me to look at things with remarkable clarity. I sat by the water and prayed for what seemed like days. Now, I'm not some bible thumping preacher who stands above the pulpit telling anyone who'll listen that the world is going to end soon and the ways of the unenlightened will fuel the fires of hell. Shit, I don't care if you drink. I care if I drink! I could get in touch with God as I understood God.

A major mortgage company in Houston had agreed to finance five houses for me. I had the option to start a construction business on my own or a window company. I didn't know as much about the window business as I knew about the construction business. I asked God for the right answer. I guess he told me which way to turn. It was never a voice or some omnipresent mythical figure directing me from the sky. I just knew and I knew where the wisdom came from. The difference between success and failure is that the successful man makes more right decisions than wrong decisions. Pretty simple, but you'd be surprised how many smart people cannot figure that out.

In 1979, Champion Window Company had been running for close to five years. Dick Wallrath had been distributing windows exclusively for the first few years of the company's existence. The company began manufacturing windows sometime in 1978. The profit train halted when the company expanded into manufacturing. A man named Ralph Zuckerberg answered a window salesman's ad in the Houston paper. Ralph Zuckerberg was born in 1950 and grew up in Providence, Rhode Island. Ralph went to the University of Arkansas on a football scholarship to play defensive lineman. In those days, tackles and ends split duty in the trenches. Ralph wound up getting hurt in his second year and lost his free ride. It didn't matter much because Ralph graduated in two years and made a great deal of money before he reached the age of twenty-one.

After their initial interview failed to seal a relationship, a second interview with Dick Wallrath was arranged. The job had already been offered to Ralph after the first interview, but no agreement had been reached. Dick Wallrath was not overjoyed to wait for anyone to let HIM know if they wanted to work for Champion Window Company. Dick Wallrath placed the window sales ad that Ralph first inquired about. Dick Wallrath conducted the interview and Dick Wallrath would decide which names filled the payroll sheets of his company. Ralph Zuckerberg traveled back East for a visit and some time to reflect about his next career decision.

During the second interview, Dick and Ralph were interrupted by a marketing call that somehow got through to Dick's office. Dick excused himself politely and then proceeded to unleash a profane tirade that would have made Attila the Hun blush. Dick called the telemarketer every derogatory cliché written, discussed or mentioned in modern times. Finally, Dick instructed the man to take a hike and hung up. Ralph took in the phone display, slowly folded his notebook and stood up.

"Mr. Wallrath," Ralph began. "I do not need this job and I certainly do not want to subject myself to this every day. Thank you for the job offer, but I decline. I am Jewish and you offend me."

Dick stood up as well and grabbed Ralph by the tie. Dick was not the biggest guy around, but he had a temper and he was one strong sonofabitch. Dick pulled Ralph up and over the top of his desk. They were now eye to eye. Dick spoke first.

"Boy, don't ever forget this." Wallrath barked within a few inches of Zuckerberg's face. "I am not prejudiced against anybody. I hate everybody equally."

Ralph sat back down, smiled and took the job. The match worked well. Ralph agreed to sell windows for the company but first wanted to work inside the factory to learn more about the products he was going to be selling. Ralph learned three things inside the factory. First he learned that most of the employees were drinking on the job. Secondly, most of the employees were doing drugs on the job. Thirdly, most of the employees were screwing the company in one form or the other. Employees were having friends punch their time cards without showing up. Breaks were extended. Fights were common on the premises. Raw materials disappeared regularly. Quality controls were non-existent. Products were going out late. The windows themselves were made well, but there were few checks and

71

balances on the process.

After six months, Ralph Zuckerberg was made Sales Manager. Within the next year, the entire corporate management would be changed. Personnel changes throughout the company put Champion Window Company on a fast track to success. Ralph Zuckerberg, eventually became President of the company and under Dick Wallrath's leadership and charisma, the revamped management team helped build the largest independent window company in Texas.

Ralph Zuckerberg: Dick Wallrath had visions of the business that simply needed the right team in place to get him there. If ever there was a man that enjoyed being a Texan, it was Dick Wallrath. I had that East Coast mentality of cost-efficiency at any cost. Dick had the iron hand that allowed me to execute the plans necessary to take Champion Window Company to much higher levels. Dick made the tough decisions that had to be made. One of the greatest strengths that Dick has always possessed involved the outside perception of his intelligence. Dick found a way to allow everyone to think he had this Texas mean streak and a double dose of stubborn Texas arrogance, which he did possess, but the brilliance of his methods were the most obvious. Dick gave off the impression that he was country dumb or Dixie blind. He was neither. Dick is one of the most intelligent businessmen I have known and his intuition to play on his image has been nothing short of brilliant.

I think one of the reasons that Dick was an angry man at times had to do with his alcoholism. Hell, I'm not a psychologist, but I believe that many alcoholics want to drink and they are angry that they have been picked to be the ones who cannot drink. That may be dime store psychology, but if there was any truth whatsoever to that theory, Dick made it work for him. The crew at Champion was afraid of Dick but they loved his ass. They wanted to work for a character like Dick Wallrath.

The beliefs of Dick Wallrath came from simple plans. This was Texas. Even the smallest customer of Champion Window Company in Texas did not deserve to be treated any differently than the largest home builder in Houston or the premier residential track builder in San Antonio. Dick didn't care if a customer came into the office sales floor with pig shit on his nose. That customer had better be dealt with politely, courteously and promptly or Mr. Wallrath had no problem to call that employee out to task. There was no border side to the boss. Dick Wallrath never straddled a fence. He jumped right up and took a stand. The old cliché, "if you don't stand for something, you'll fall for everything" never branded Mr. Wallrath.

On one occasion, during an excessively hot spell one summer, Champion had an oversized order to get out under the gun. Ralph and many others came in over a Saturday and Sunday, staying well into the night on Sunday. The task was to finish about sixty hours of work in less than two days. The air-conditioning in the office had broken, The HVAC repairmen could not get to Champion until Monday morning. Ralph and his group worked into the night, They had stripped down to their underwear, brought in some beer, some well-rolled Mexican weed and some other assorted artificial stimulants that were at best not allowed anywhere near the premises on regular business days and at worst, were flat out illegal. It was very late on Sunday night and Dick Wallrath happened by his plant and wondered what all the commotion inside was all about. Dick opened the door to the conference room and the place froze up. Dick stared at the conference table with a couple dozen empty beer cans, ash trays filled with joints and the half-naked staff scattered around like drunks at an all night fraternity party. Dick asked his corporate Chief Executive Officer what was going on?

"We are working." Ralph's reply was short.

Dick stood there and continued to eyeball the room. After Ralph's answer sunk in, Dick turned and left the building. He never mentioned the evening again. No one was chastised. No one was grilled or asked to explain the actions of that evening. The project was completed. The plans were drawn up on time and the materials were delivered. Loyalty is not an abstract concept. Men and women are drawn to individuals who skate on the edge not by duplicity or design but by instinct and heart.

Ralph Zuckerberg: I can recall one day in late 1986 or early 1987. I was called to the main sales desk in the lobby of our plant to mediate an exchange that had escalated to a level that the sales person could not cope with the problem. The sales manager on the floor that day, also failed to control the situation. I came out of my office, unhappy that I had to mediate the discussion but willing to listen carefully to fully understand the issues. I was met by a mountain of a man. The day's journey to our plant to pick up his order left him smelling like a locker room in July. The Hungarian builder had been told to arrive on that particular day to pick up his order. Some builders saved the freight bill by picking up their orders. The windows in question were not in stock. He had been told something different and he was legitimately pissed off. I would have been really pissed off if the shoes were reversed. It happens. We would have made the guy his windows on the spot, but he chose a different path to follow. When I arrived to inquire about the problem, he asked who I was? When he was informed that I was the company President, he wondered why a Jew, sonofabitch was put in charge of the company. I explained to him that we could make his windows if he calmed down. That apparently, was never going to occur. He wanted to know why Hitler never finished the job? I had enough and resigned myself that this was not going to be a person that we wanted to do business with. Before I could get the thought out of my mind, I caught a glimpse of Dick Wallrath literally leaping over a desk with a pickaxe handle in his hand. All one hundred fifty pounds of that man came over the desk line like a damn rhino with a gonad infection. Dick shoved that axe handle up under the man's chin, which was considerably higher than his own, and extended an invitation for them to settle the matter in the parking lot. Dick proceeded to explain how they would resolve the matter and that solution boiled down to one simple statement. Dick told the irate customer that if he raised his hand one time, Dick would kill him. The statement wasn't a threat, it was a fact. Size left the equation from that moment on. A man must be able to ascertain what lies within a man's eyes and what lies within a man's heart when the fanfare is over. When the tactical lip service is not happening and a physical confrontation is inevitable, the eyes give away everything. The big Hungarian wanted nothing to do with the little German.

Dick Wallrath: The first year was rough. I know that I am not telling a single businessman or woman that has started an independent business anything new. The first year or two in a new business is hell. I worked sixteen or eighteen hour days to make less than half the money I had made as a window salesman. Great move, huh? When I remembered back to the speech by Richard Gilmour LeTourneau, I was reminded of my own relationship with

God. I told God that I was going to give him the business to run for awhile. I would give twenty percent of everything I made to charity. My company grew by one million dollars that next year and I began to acquire the people necessary to grow substantially each year and maintain the same quality and service that made smaller companies so appealing.

During the first three years, my CPA's, bankers and attorneys told me that I didn't have enough money to finance the rapid growth that I envisioned. I had made a reputation for paying my bills by the tenth of each month and my suppliers could set their watches to my checks. When times arose that made a payment late, I always called to inform the supplier that the check would be late and I specified how late. There was never anything but support from these companies. I have always put my business up front and on the table. When my business was rolling, the first dollars were ALWAYS sent to the suppliers and the banks. When times were tough, those suppliers and banks came through like a slow curveball floating right down to the middle of the plate. While my own agreement with God has provided funding to various agencies and charities, the agreement has come full circle with me and my own spirituality has grown immeasurably.

Andy Vavra: To say that Dick Wallrath has a unique handle on his own business is like saying that Mike Tyson brought an unusual twist to professional boxing. I am not certain that biting off body parts is a common practice taught in gyms across the country. But, hell, he did what he thought he had to. I had been selling windows and working in the manufacturing plant at Champion for a few years when I can recall the most unusual settlement I had ever been associated with. We had a builder in the Houston area, near Galveston, that had placed a very large order for windows to a track home site that had at least two dozen homes under construction. We had delivered more than half the windows for those homes but had not received any money for the products. Repeated calls to the firm were ignored until the President of the company finally returned one of our calls. The comptroller at Champion was informed by the President of the home builder in question that they were in arrears to numerous firms and that Champion was not high on the list of creditors. The likely scenario had the company filing bankruptcy and stiffing all the suppliers. A new company would emerge and assume the debt at a fraction of the original cost and the builder would come out smelling sweeter than a rose pedal on a lemon wedge. The builder almost reveled in his predicament.

The problem had to be brought to Dick's attention. When the facts were confirmed and the builder relayed the same sarcastic glee to Mr. Wallrath, a solution to the problem would not be long in coming. Dick hopped in his Cadillac and brought me along. We drove down to the Galveston construction site, where more than a dozen homes were at various stages of completion. Another dozen or more were already tracked out on the property. A lone security guard was weary when Dick barely gave him a glance at the entrance to the property. The houses under construction all had Champion Windows installed. Dick pulled the car to a halt and got out without saying a word. I simply observed. Dick Wallrath picked up a two by four that was maybe eight feet long. He proceeded to enter the first home under construction. Dick took that length of wood and smashed out every single window in that house, including the skylight in the kitchen. When he emerged from the house, the sound of shattering glass still resonated in the air. Dick had a look of fulfillment in his eyes and a shit-ass Texas grin on his face. "No one is going to use those damn windows if I don't get paid for them!"

The exercise was repeated in every house on the property. The security guard came up to the Cadillac after the commotion of the first house. The guard suggested to Dick that he leave the property immediately. Dick took out a twelve-gauge shotgun and told the security guard to sit his ass down and shut his Gosh darn mouth. Dick then broke up the remainder of the homes under construction that had used Champion Windows. He made certain that the only part of the houses he touched were the windows. We drove back to Houston and Dick never mentioned it to the staff at Champion. Everyone knew. The builder eventually called back and reordered the entire project. The delivery was made only after the original invoice and the subsequent invoice were paid in advance.

The brashness and audacity that Dick Wallrath brought to every turn in his life only gained strength through his battle with alcohol. The demons of alcohol were like an opponent that preyed upon the weak. Those demons found a stellar foe in Dick Wallrath, as did anyone else that underestimated Dick's resolve and willingness to do whatever was necessary to build his business into the enterprise that he envisioned. During the early days of Champion Window Company, the repeated break-ins at the plant were uncommonly brazen and the additional security had not stopped the problem. Dick was still relatively small and did not have the financial where with all to support a specific security force. Bigger fences, tougher locks and added lighting did not do the trick. The next available solution to the problem was elementary to the company founder. Dick decided he would sleep at the plant and thwart any break-ins on his own. Recently divorced, the move to the back of the plant was a personal financial move as well.

Ralph Zuckerberg: Dick was fed up with the break-ins. I had not come to work for Dick, yet. The word got around the industry pretty fast. On one particular night, two African-American males broke into the plant offices. The break-in was mainly a quest for office equipment and if they got lucky, some cash. The alarm went off and woke Dick up. It was very late. Dick grabbed a double-barreled sawed off shotgun and headed for the offices. Inside the offices, two men were disconnecting office machinery in preparation for their departure. The presence of Dick startled one into flight. The other chose to move toward Dick with a tire tool. That was the last time he moved toward anyone. I believe that night changed Dick. I believe that Dick may have understood his maturation and some additional appreciation for the principles found in his twelve step program, to be a direct result of his decision to take a life in defense of his property. There were no charges filed against Dick. The police ruled the shooting a justifiable homicide and praised Dick for his actions in the heat of an invasion. The slain intruder had contraband from numerous Houston home invasions in his vehicle. In Texas, we carry guns as a way of life. If any individual chooses to pursue a life of breaking and entering Texas businesses, then the acute awareness of those dangers had better be foremost in the mind of that individual or the chances of that person ever collecting a social security check would become extremely slim.

Business took the two unlikely partners into some strange arenas. Here, on one hand, was the East Coast, city slicker, college educated and schooled in the world and corporate warfare. On the other hand, stood a Texan with definitive social awareness issues. Dick Wallrath never met a politically correct cliché or acronym that he didn't ignore. Dick never singled out one particular target to offend. He believed in spreading the wealth out equally and that was particularly evident in the negotiations with the many suppliers of

Champion Window Company.

Ralph Zuckerberg: There has always been a great deal of corruption in business and the window business was no exception. Let me give you an example. Say one representative from a glass supplier came to my office. He had done his homework and knew that at Champion Window Company, we bought in excess of eighteen million dollars in glass each calendar year. Normally, we split that up among a few suppliers. Now, one company came to me and proposed that if we purchased all of our glass from his company, that company would send me a penny per square foot as a stipend to my house. In other words, they were bribing me to purchase everything from one company and that bribe could amount to a substantial amount of money for me. Who would know? Now, I always made more money than I dreamed of because Dick knew how to produce results and that was through incentives. I was not about to steal from myself. Many times inside a corporate boardroom, I would be in a meeting with a particular supplier and I played the game to the hilt. I asked them to be discreet beyond reproach. I insisted that they not offer me any stipend. (The stern insistence accompanied by a wink and an understanding.) Dick's reputation preceded him everywhere. I told the suppliers that they should know his reputation and that I was not in a position to purchase on an exclusive basis. Dick would barge into the boardroom on cue and accuse me of stealing money with the supplier. Dick would rant about Jew this and Jew that (referring to me). He would announce that he knew I was stealing money through the company I was meeting with. Dick was very intimidating. The cowboy hat and the boots were only the tip of the menace. Dick's stern gray stare was unnerving. The company invariably winced at his charade. They pleaded their case and assured Mr.

Wallrath that nothing of the kind was going on. To make certain that Mr. Wallrath accepted their explanation, the price levels of their products hit the bottom. Dick and I played that game many times.

Champion Window Company grew in size, stature and influence within the industry basically because Dick Wallrath insisted that be the case. It became very clear to anyone that chose to do business with Champion or any company that Champion chose to include within their conquest of the window industry, that Mr. Wallrath was not a man to be trifled with. The employees of Champion Window Company were given a hands-on lesson on the art of passion and the connection of commitment.

Part of the Wallrath style was to reward the employees of his company in different ways. In late 1986, Mr. Wallrath decided to take the entire sales force bass fishing in Mexico. The destination was a resort called Lago Vista in Lake Guerrero, Mexico, some eight or nine hours by car from Houston. The fishing lodge was owned by a banker from Brownsville, Texas named Mr. Duncan. Dick drove one vehicle and was to be followed by a small caravan of the remaining sales staff. Ralph accompanied Dick in his vehicle.

Ralph Zuckerberg: Driving with Dick was an experience that may have precluded anyone from giving up alcohol. Not only was a seatbelt a necessity, a NASCAR Hans device, a full face helmet and a King James Bible were a good idea. Dick Wallrath drove like he was tempting the boundaries of his own mortality. The passenger was simply unlucky, uniniti-ated, ill-advised and pretty much in a constant state of prayer that some form of motorized authority would eventually slow the boss down. Far be it from us to suggest that perhaps it was wise to reduce the average traveling speed to the two digit framework. Obsessive personalities tend to pursue work, recreation and family with a frenzied fervor that they are born with.

Dick and Ralph arrived in Mexico by the grace of God. Rain followed them from Houston and continued throughout the hours of trepidation. The other salesman arrived some time after Dick and Ralph found the lodge. Everyone was dog-tired and hungry. The owner of the lodge was a high-roller type and very impressed with himself, his string of fishing lodges and the high-powered business clients that frequently employed his locations. The late evening meal upon their arrival was somewhat less than what Dick Wallrath imagined the cost to include. The rain continued and Dick and the others went to bed, disappointed with the meal, but certain that the hour and late arrival spawned the quality.

The next morning, the rain continued. Dick Wallrath had become a man of habit. After his sobriety, Dick had embarked on a regimen of physical fitness and eating his way. Dick worked out every day and decided to eat one meal per day. His evening meal was very important to him. He ate whatever he desired and learned to appreciate good food and plenty of it. On the first rainy morning of the fishing expedition, Dick noticed that the breakfast served to his staff was less than satisfactory. Many of the guys simply pushed the plates away discreetly, not wanting to offend Dick and his generosity. Some of the guys went out fishing in the rain. Some stayed in the lodge, played cards, drank tequila shots and smoked cigars. The sales staff did not hide the drinking from Dick. The Wallrath style said, do what you want. He didn't care if his staff drank tequila, chased hookers or dressed up like Tinkerbell. They had earned the time off and he was there to help them enjoy it. The lunch proved to be a carbon copy of the previous meals.

At dinner, most of the sales force arrived well-lubricated and the quality of their fare was not an issue to focus upon. Retiring back to the deck on the second floor was a bigger priority. The recurring card game, an endless supply of some potent Mescal and a variety of foreign cannabis were the more important aspects of the vacation. Dick took issue with the evening meal. While the staff had retired upstairs, Dick confronted Mr. Duncan about a full refund for the short stay. Mr. Wallrath was not going to pay for what he called the same garbage they throw into a swine pen. Mr. Duncan and Mr. Wallrath disagreed vehemently about the quality of the meals and the general tone of the discussion deteriorated quickly. Ralph was summoned from upstairs to mediate an argument that had escalated into something much worse.

Ralph Zuckerberg: I pulled some of my bigger boys from the upstairs deck and we went downstairs to literally save Mr. Duncan. I knew what Dick was capable of and this had replay written all over it. Dick treated you fairly and expected the same. When that failed to occur, Mr. Wallrath had no issue with going after you. This was a Texas mentality. When someone disrespected you and tried to take advantage of you, then the courtroom was the last place the matter would be decided. The first place was always the end of an iron fist. Now, Mr. Duncan was a mouthy prick to begin with. When we arrived in the dining room, Dick had Mr. Duncan pinned against the wall. Mr. Duncan was turning an alarming shade of blue. Dick's grip was literally pushing through the man's neck. It took three of us to pull Dick away from the breathless host. I am certain that Dick wanted to kill the guy, but the consequences of that happening demanded some quick action.

We finally got Dick out of the lodge and into his vehicle. After screaming to Dick about the Mexican jail system and the illegal substances the Champion sales force had been consuming, the issue was not a refund or the lousy food. The issue was getting back to the border before Mr. Duncan could rally the Mexican Federalies into locking our sorry asses up for a decade or two. We did make it back to the border before the authorities reached our convoy. Dick didn't pass judgement on the choices his sales staff made as to their own methods of relaxation. Dick had a Western Sheriff's code of what was right and what was wrong. If you worked for Dick and handled yourself like a man, then your choices were none of his business. When those actions took an ominous turn then you were working elsewhere. The staff loved that about Dick. He was a bubbling volcano that spewed a little smoke all the time and exploded every now and then. What you saw with Dick Wallrath is what you got. There was never a hypocritical bone in Dick's body. One minute you loved him and the next minute, you cringed about what came out of his mouth. At meetings up North, he may have referred to a business proposal as "freaking Yankee bullshit." Dick sat ten steps to the right of Rush Limbaugh and if you were offended by his references, then that was your freaking problem. The off-beat comments never were directed as a personal attack. Dick never searched for the right way to say something. He took his stand and said what he meant. Dick was the father that I never had and captured that unabashed honesty that went out the window when lawsuits replaced personal responsibilities.

The window business flourished. Champion Window Company was responsible for the majority of residential new construction windows in the greater Houston area by the mid-nineties. A lion's share of the market had been carved into the San Antonio residential new construction growth curve. Champion Window Company branched out into the Dallas market as well. A second manufacturing plant and distribution center was opened in Las Vegas as the company's business swelled. Ralph Zuckerberg and Dick Wallrath surveyed the growth potential in Las Vegas and made the move during the early nineties. The Las Vegas venture included a complete new manufacturing facility, distribution warehouse and sales force. Ralph and Dick physically set up the shop in Nevada and for reasons beyond the plant, spent much more time than necessary in Sin City.

The Las Vegas operation had issues from the outset. The plant and distribution center was located on Polaris Drive behind Caesar's Palace. The workforce in Las Vegas proved to be less than cost effective.

Ralph Zuckerberg: We had a frightful time getting a workforce in place. The union issues were disconcerting. It was obvious that certain people did not want us to do business in Las Vegas. Why would anyone want to work a hard shift in a window factory for good wages when they could walk around an air-conditioned hotel, clean ashtrays and earn twelve dollars per hour. We had to apply for a license every time we farted. I told Dick one day, that we were chasing dollars with nickels.

After only eighteen months in Las Vegas, Champion Window Company headed back to Houston. The equipment was sold for eighty cents on the dollar and Dick Wallrath was happy to take it. Life in Las Vegas had taught Champion's founder and Champion's President two lessons. First, there were way too many potential nieces in Las Vegas.

Secondly, security, financial conservation and the advancement of the home life do not flourish from the craps table at the Rio Hotel.

In 1999, Champion Window Company was sold. Dick Wallrath retained 22% of the business and remained on the Board of Directors. His active role in the company's day to day business had ended. The firm was in equal parts purchased by an investment banker, Sanders, Morris and Harris. The second equal partner was Equus, a venture capitalist. The company in 2005 should gross over one-hundred million dollars in window sales. Dick Wallrath walked away from the company he founded and turned his good fortune into the statement of his existence. Mogul and philanthropist were euphemisms tossed around like confetti at a ticker-tape parade. Dick Wallrath was never concerned with titles or accolades. Dick turned to the business of aiding many young lives in a positive manner. Dick believed that education was the one necessary tool to achieve success. A power greater than he, laid down the path long ago. Dick Wallrath took the milestones in his life as the markers on a path that would certainly define the reason he was given the opportunity to succeed. Success was not about the acquisition of material wealth, real estate, Ferraris, yachts or exclusive club memberships. Success was the acquisition of accomplishment. Success for Dick Wallrath was the ability to level the playing field for those who couldn't get close to the game. He not only brought them down to the field, he put them in the game. More than three decades had passed since Dick Wallrath had turned his unmanageable life over to a power greater than himself. Dick trusted God, as he understood God, to guide him home.

CHAPTER 6

Chapter Six...Caitlin Olivia Lee Dalton

January 2, 2004

Dear Mr. Wallrath,

My name is Caitlin Dalton. I received a Houston Livestock Show and Rodeo Scholarship in the summer of 2003 through my local 4-H club. Sir, I must apologize. Today, while I was sorting some paperwork in my file box, I came across your name and address as my Houston donor. I am so sorry, sir. I was under the impression that I was to send the appreciation letters to Dr. Quarles. I can only offer you my sincere apologies and hope you continue to support the 4-H programs for years to come. This is supposed to be a progress letter, so despite my embarrassment, I will attempt to make it a good one.

I am currently attending Texas Tech University. I will be classified as a sophomore this spring. I chose to attend the university here for several reasons. First, my father is an assistant professor here. The university also has an excellent reputation for having nearly all of its applying students accepted to the veterinary school. Since I eventually hope to become an equine specialist, that characteristic of Texas Tech was very important to me. I know that I will receive an excellent agricultural education here.

I have a double major in Animal Science and Russian. Animal Science is definitely the best choice for me. Ever since I was a little girl, I have been very good with animals. I love horses and a career in equine medicine seems to be the next natural step. As for my Russian major, I love foreign languages. I am fluent in German and wanted a language that would be a formidable challenge. I certainly found it. After I receive my two degrees and graduate, I hope to volunteer for two years in the Peace Corps as an agricultural worker. A background in agriculture and language opens endless possibilities for careers and connections in numerous fields.

This fall I took on fourteen hours and a part-time job. Most of my classes were not difficult but required a great deal of study time. My grades were all A's except for my Chemistry 1301 class. Even though I studied more for that class than any other class, it seems that an A was not within my reach. I enrolled to take nineteen hours for the spring semester. It will be a big load, but I feel like I can handle it. Having that many hours will put me at a Junior level next fall. The reason that I am taking so many hours is to be able to try out for Masked Rider, Tech's most recognizable symbol. Tryouts are held every spring. This spring, I do not have enough hours to be eligible. Next spring though, I will be ready. Even if I do not make it, then at least I know I had tried.

As for extracurricular activities, I have been active in several clubs. I rushed and became a member of Sigma Alpha. SA is a professional sorority in which at least eighty percent of the members are Ag majors. Next semester I hope to participate in the Block and Bridle Club. B & B is an organization within the Ag college that does numerous fundraisers and events for charities throughout the year. As a Russian major, I participated in the Russian Club as well. This fall, it was mainly a series of lectures but this summer we are planning a trip to Saint Petersburg. There we will be able to earn six hours credit from Saint Petersburg University. I know that all of this sounds like a full plate, but I know that I can juggle all these endeavors to become a well-rounded, ready for the world person.

Thank you so much for your support of 4-H members as they continue on with their dreams through college. I cannot express to you how grateful I am that you are so generous. Thank you and the Houston Livestock Show and Rodeo so much for your incredible generosity towards today's youth. Your commitment to us is appreciated much more than can be expressed. Without organizations and individuals willing to do what you are doing, many people would not be able to attend college. Many more would have tremendous difficulty getting through college. I hope that in the future you will continue to support 4-H Round-Up Scholars and their endeavors to "make the best better." Thank you again. Have a Happy New Year!

Sincerely,

Caitie Dalton

A Sample of a Scholarship Award Recipient and Their Background, Caitlin Olivia Lee Dalton.

4-H Projects...

Horse (1995-2003)

1) Raised six horses including two show foals born to my broodmare.

2) Dedicated 2100 hours to the project.

3) Learned about anatomy, nutrition, reproduction, training, health, riding, breeding, stud selection, and mare care.

4) Presented horse related public speaking and demonstrations for seven years.

5) Presented in 4-H Horse Judging and Quiz Bowl Team for three years.

Sheep (1997-2003)

1) Raised fourteen sheep for show over five years.

2) Presented sheep related talks and methods demonstrations over five years.

3) Participated on Wool Judging Team.

4) Participated in Natural Fibers Contest.

Photography (1995-2003)

1) Exhibited for eight years.

2) Led a Junior Photography Class for two years and four photography workshops for children 9-13 years old.

3) Helped to develop the first District Photography Contest for D2.

4) Served as school photographer and sports photographer for local paper for two years,

learning about getting the right shot for the most impact.

Clothing (1995-2003)

1) Exhibited seven years and participated in thirteen project workshops.

2) Constructed 32 garments over seven years. Constructed approximately 100 other articles cobering more than 700 hours.

3) State Fashion Board member for two years.

4) Served as Fashion Show Narrator.

Volunteer (1999-2003)

1) Helped set up 4-H clubs on Fort Hood Army Base.

2) Volunteered at San Antonio Horse Judging Competition.

3) Started, led and developed curriculum for an after school 4-H program for children in a day care center.

4) Volunteered as a tour guide at the San Antonio Livestock Exposition.

5) Made aprons and awards for three years for Food Show.

6) Developed and led 12 meetings for the Horseless Horse 4-H Project.

7) Began a now annual necessities drive for a local food bank that has raised over $1000.

Caitlin Dalton continued,

Elected Appointed (1999-2003)

1) President of the Horse Club, Coryell County.

2) Vice-President of Southwest Frenship 4-H Club, Lubbock County.

3) Council Representative, Southwest Friendship 4-H Club, Lubbock County.

4) Council Representative, Hay Valley 4-H Club, Coryell County.

5) Council reporter, Coryell County.

6) Reporter and Secretary for Lubbock County 4-H Council

7) Community Service Chair, Coryell County.

Outside Honors

1) National Honor Society (2001-2003)

2) After School Tutor (2001-2003)

3) Tennis Team Member (1999-2002)

4) Live Oak Baptist Church (1998-2002)

5) FFA Dairy judging Team (1999-2001)

6) Horse Judging Team (1999-2001)

CHAPTER 7

Dick and Patsy

Three Texas Friends... World Champion bull rider Bobby Steiner, Texas Governer Rick Perry and Dick Wallrath

Patsy Murphy, President Bush, and Dick Wallrath

Dina Denise Wallrath Robertson
1961-1993

Dick Wallrath and Texas FFA Foundation Executive Director Aaron Alejandro

2005 Texas FFA Convention
Honoring Dick Wallrath... Lubbock, Texas

Author Jim Pomerantz, Champion Ranch cattle manager Tuffy Loftin, Dick Wallrath, Dick's daughter Pam Wallrath Dolenz, Patsy Murphy, and Aaron Alejandro (far right)

Thank You for supporting
the Young People of the Texas FFA

Chapter Seven...Patsy Murphy

The loud voice in the background was unmistakable. Charles Murphy was a truck driver, haul-
ing gas around Tyler, Texas in an eighteen-wheel rig. Charles "Charlie" Murphy grew up in the

Louisiana country, got married young and provided for his family in the blue-collar tradition of

middle-class America. A trip to the hospital during the middle of the night to attend to his intox-

icated daughter did not sit well with the part-time Baptist preacher. Eventually, the staff had to

forcibly remove the enraged father from the hospital.

Patsy Murphy had no direction during high school in Tyler, Texas. She had no dis-

cernible idea of why she had landed on this earth. One thing she did know, however, was

that the sooner she was out of the house on her own, the better her life would have to

become. The sixteen-year old high school junior had been drinking on this night. There

was a bottle of open liquor in the car and most of it was inside Patsy by the time another

drunk driver blew a stop sign. The other vehicle had been traveling without any headlights.

It was nearly two in the morning. The two cars collided into a sea of twisted metal. The

liquor bottle inside Patsy's car burst and now the frightened driver had been drenched in a

shower of whiskey. An emergency room doctor who knew the Murphy family shielded

Patsy from the police. They had, after all, focused on the other drunk driver who happened

to run the intersection without lights. While the local police focused on the other driver,

Patsy focused on her father, storming down the hospital corridor. Within the most contra-

dictory terms, Patsy's introduction to blackouts would be a memorable experience.

Patsy Murphy was born in Shreveport, Louisiana. The family moved to Fort Worth soon

after Patsy was born and moved again to Tyler before she reached the age of six. Pasty

went through school in Tyler. One brother and one sister were much older and although

Patsy admired her older sister, their contact was minimal due to the eight-year difference in age. Getting out of the house was Patsy's sole goal after high school. She married the same year. Her new husband joined the Navy and shipped out for Vietnam some nine months after they were married. It was 1970. Patsy was alone, out of the house and about to discover she had a great deal to learn about growing up.

Divorce followed quickly. Her husband was still in Vietnam when they divorced. A move to New Orleans did not work out. Another marriage followed. The couple moved to Houston soon after they were married.

Patsy Murphy: I remember my first encounters with alcohol, or should I say that I remember parts of those experiences. I used to get drunk, drunk. I always got to the point where I was throwing up. Now, in my convoluted mind, I figured that if I wasn't very good at drinking then I would certainly be much better at handling narcotics. While my second husband and I were still in Tyler, I had taken to getting major migraine headaches. After the prescriptions proved effective, I rushed to have them refilled much sooner than the bottle called for. Within a very short period of time, my doctors revoked the prescriptions explaining that the pills could lead to addiction and that I would be better off with some over the counter medication. I was already addicted to the prescribed painkillers. My husband at the time envisioned himself as a wanna-be criminal. At six foot four and three-hundred fifty pounds, he was an intimidating presence. His connections made it simple for me to score the pills I needed. Another offshoot of his weight was his ability to obtain diet pills. I would be buzzing for days on the pills prescribed for my husband's weight control issues.

Our sphere of friends continued to get seedier. We had biker friends and the group had now gotten into LSD. My first experience with LSD came on a camping trip. That was my first and last camping trip. The drug experience was scary but I looked at it like riding a horse. Once you get thrown, you have to get back up on that horse as soon as you can. The camping thing was not for me. Ironic, sometimes when I think back to those days. I was more adamant about not camping again than I was about not tripping again. My second husband and I moved to Houston where the drug use escalated.

Patsy had always been able to maintain her own jobs and gain some independence with her own money and her own identity. Her friends were selling some marijuana and cocaine. Patsy found the pleasure in snorting cocaine and snorting heroin. The needles scared her to death, but sending the product up her nose was less invasive and equally as satisfying. In between jobs in Houston, Patsy went to work for her sister and her husband at the Snowflake Bakery in Houston. She agreed to help them out starting a new business. Dishing out donuts to stoned hippies and overweight business types was not the evolution-ary progression that Patsy had imagined, but it worked for a short stop. The drugs were ongoing. Alcohol made life difficult for Patsy to function in. There were more blackouts and more totaled cars. With drugs, life was manageable or at least that appeared to be the case.

The year was 1975. On one morning, a well-dressed man entered the donut shop and began to make small talk with Patsy. The man was Dick Wallrath. Dick was the owner of a young, growing window company. Patsy remembered that Dick was very handsome and cocky. They spoke on that first meeting about real jobs and what Patsy enjoyed doing. Patsy told Dick that she was a bookkeeper and a good one. The donut gig was simply to help out family. Dick mentioned that he was looking for a bookkeeper for his window company, which was located near the donut shop. They agreed to meet to discuss the position. They came to terms quickly. Patsy started working for Champion Windows in 1975. She was still married. Dick was still married. Patsy was drinking and doing drugs. Dick was sober. Near the end of their first meeting, Dick walked to the door of the donut shop, turned back to Patsy and asked her of she had ever been to Acapulco? Patsy answered that she had never been to Acapulco. Dick told her that he would take her there someday.

Patsy Murphy: Champion Window Company had been open a little more than one year when I went to work for Dick Wallrath. I was to start on a Monday. Dick fired his bookkeeper on Friday during the week prior to my first day. When I got to Champion, I sat on Coke cases for a chair and pulled out a mountain of quarterly reports that had not been filled out and filed. I had been fortunate enough to work for a small construction company in Tyler for a few years, where the owner taught me a great deal about running the books for an independent company. This experience was invaluable to Dick Wallrath, to Champion Window Company and that combined with Dick's not so subtle social interest in me was just what the doctor ordered.

The window company had its growing pains as did the relationship that Dick and Patsy would eventually develop. Systematic bonding grew inside the company between Patsy and some of the other employees. The usual routine had them going out after work for an evening of winding down and getting loaded. Many of the employees of the company attended those gatherings. Dick never joined the outings. Patsy was unaware of Dick's sobriety and his experiences with the Twelve-Step Program. Patsy remembered the attempts to get Dick to smoke pot or loosen up. He was unaware of her spiraling problem with substance abuse, but Patsy was not shy about drinking around Dick. The relationship grew quickly from a business relationship. Both were still married but both knew their marriages would not last much longer.

As the business and personal relationship meshed, it became obvious that Patsy was having problems on some isolated mornings due to a massive hangover or the ill effects lingering from an evening of cocaine use. The colorless cheeks and lost eyes were the all too familiar warning lights that Dick had been witnessing in meetings for more than five years. Patsy's second marriage was deteriorating quickly. Her second husband was unaware of the slippery slope his wife was following. He facilitated the drug use and they both drank and consumed drugs together. The only remaining bond between Patsy and her husband was glued to the substance abuse. Patsy's parents had moved back to Louisiana during the latter stages of her second marriage. The fear factor associated with becoming loaded around her parents was now gone. Although Patsy resided with her husband and did not live with her parents, the need for their tacit approval never waned. Distance became an enabler. It was after a multitude of comatose mornings, that Dick brought Patsy to her first Twelve-Step meeting.

Patsy Murphy: I had those early meetings pegged tighter than a fat lady's stubby foot wedged inside a size six red pump. I was twenty-seven years old and those people at the Twelve Step meetings were older than God. They had no problem giving up living, but I sure as hell was not about to join them. They needed that Twelve Step jive and I did not! Dick knew I had a problem, but you can only lead the horse to water. You cannot force him to drink. Hell, I went high to more than half of the meetings I attended during those introductory days.

Dick's marriage ended and Patsy's marriage ended at roughly the same time. The reasons were unrelated to their ongoing relationship or at the least, their relationship was only problematic to the underlying differences between Dick and his first wife and the underlying differences between Patsy and her second husband. As can be the case, divorce settlements proved long and arduous. The relationship between Patsy and her husband clashed in the courtroom, but facilitated each other's need to get loaded. Patsy continued to visit her separated husband's home for the sole purpose of getting high. On a Fourth of July weekend, Patsy partied at the home of her second husband. The party lasted three days. Patsy overdosed on a combination of cocaine, heroin and an unknown quantity of amphetamines. Patsy had no food or nourishment for three days. Her body weight had dropped to less than ninety pounds. Her clothes hung on her frame like an oversized shirt on a wire hanger.

Dick somehow tracked Patsy down towards the end of that holiday weekend. The assistant bookkeeper at Champion Window Company had screwed up the monthly billing cycle and Dick was frantic about not having any money coming in. Dick was a man that was anal about paying his bills on time. When it appeared that timely record was in jeopardy, Dick begged Patsy to come in during the holiday and fix the billing cycle. Dick Wallrath knew it was imperative to get the invoices mailed on time. Dick, at the time, was unaware of the damage Patsy had already done to her body and her mind. Patsy somehow made it into the office on Duncan Road in Houston. Dick Wallrath took one look at his bookkeeper and part-time girlfriend and gasped.

"What the hell happened to you?" Dick inquired, although he knew the answer. Patsy looked up and rolled her eyes. Through the next ten hours, Patsy managed to fix the billing cycle, organize the monthly statements and get the mailings ready for the next business day. Patsy was near a complete physical and mental breakdown. Now it was her turn. She dragged herself into Dick's office and collapsed in a chair. She was crying.

"I need your help." She knew it was time.

"I can't help you. " Dick emphatically replied.

Patsy Murphy: I knew at that moment in Dick's office that if I drank again or did drugs again, it would be the ultimate cause of my death. Now, my death was to be locked away behind bars. The thought of not being able to tell anyone that I was all right was death to me. I was scared to death for the first time in my life.

"What do you mean, you can't help me?" Patsy had just reached out to the one man who knew about the problems she was having and he told her that he couldn't help. Dick had been taking Patsy to the meetings. She never heard what was said. He had taken her to another program to dry out. Dick witnessed Patsy's immediate return to drugs and alcohol. Dick Wallrath knew about alcohol, but the drug use was another issue. He did not know enough to be the one to help Patsy. Dick called on some friends that night. Dick drove Patsy clear across Houston and Patsy stayed with some people she had met at an earlier meeting. Dick's friends were very familiar with drugs and alcohol. They fed Patsy a combination of ice cream and honey for three days. Some color came back to Patsy's cheeks. Those friends stayed through the withdrawals. Patsy was using heroin and cocaine. The cold turkey ramifications were altogether different from alcohol. Whether the drugs were ingested through the nose or through the veins, the loss to the body was dramatic.

Patsy and Dick went to meetings every night for almost two years. Patsy was an angry person during those two years. She resented the fact that she had to stop drinking and doing drugs while her ex-friends were out having the time of their lives. Patsy didn't get it. She sat through the meetings, but was what was referred to as a dry drunk. Dry drunks were people that were a hair away from their next drink. They hated the fact that they couldn't drink and everyone else could. Patsy wanted so bad to go back to drugs and alcohol. She was a bitch to be around. Dick hung in there. Patsy didn't know how to live sober, even after two years. The ever present return to drug use and alcohol use was always there. Why did she have to be the one to stop. Maybe she could handle the "bad day?" The ominous "bad day" was a day, where the alcoholic might decide to have one drink on that day. The dry drunk "bad day" was potentially every day. The dry drunk imagined the drink, but became fixated nonetheless. The dry drunk alcoholic may have been very good for six months thus rationalizing that a "bad day" had been earned. Maybe the dry drunk had lost a job or caused an automobile accident. Regardless of the reason, the dry drunk always believed that he/she had earned a drink. The dry drunk alcoholic knew that he could shut it down the next day. Patsy admitted to having a dry drunk "bad day" everyday for those first two years.

Patsy Murphy: Dick had been sober for eight or nine years at this point. I was a basket case. I wanted to do drugs so bad. I wanted to drink more than I ever wanted to drink when I was drinking. I didn't even like drinking much, but I missed it. To this day, I do not know why that man stayed around. He was sober, had his life on track and the last thing he needed was a mental case girlfriend with a hair trigger temper and a manic desire to drink her brains out. I know now, that God put the right person in my life. No one else could have handled my psychosomatic roller coaster.

I was living alone at the time. Dick and I were together, but we each had our own apartments. Thank God for that. Had Dick and I been living together, I cannot imagine how he could have put up with a full dose of twenty-four hour Patsy seven days a week. One night while alone in my apartment, I was slamming things around and feeling sorry for myself as usual. It hit me hard that night. I finally just screamed at the top of my lungs, "God help me!" I slid down the wall and rolled my knees up under my chin. I began to cry and for the first time in my life, I meant what I said. I needed God to help me. I couldn't fight this thing anymore. At that moment, a calm came over me that was like a new dress on a bright sunny morning. My lungs settled and my breath eased up. The turmoil stopped. The insanity stopped. I still didn't know what I was doing, but I knew why. I began to listen to everyone at those meetings. It was like I was there for the first time. I began to believe that I could live without drugs and alcohol. I knew that I could live without drugs and alcohol. I could have a relationship without getting high and enjoy it. Dick guided me through the program and God bless that man for standing by me when he should have packed his life away and left me staring at the taillights. No one on this earth would have stayed by me like he did.

Dick and Patsy have been together for almost thirty years. They were married for less than three years. Champion Window Company had been on a fast track to success. Dick's sons Michael and Danny were involved with the company. Ralph had just come on board and both Dick and Patsy had managed to put some sober years behind them. Marriage seemed like the natural progression of life. They talked about spending less time at the business and acted upon those wishes immediately after the wedding. The rest and relaxation did not last long. The business encountered some problems that required Dick to get fully involved again. Together, they focused on the issues at Champion. Twenty-four hours per day together in marriage was not the answer. Dick and Patsy filed for divorce two and one-half years after they got married. They moved into separate apartments again. After two weeks apart, they moved back in together, let the divorce papers take their course and have been together ever since without the formalities of marriage.

Dick always ran the window company under the same guidelines as the Twelve Step Program. Dick Wallrath did not believe in lying to promote his business, regardless of the fact that most suppliers, contractors and banks altered their own perception of the truth to best suit their individual and company needs. That practice was common in business and is more prevalent today than ever. Business is a marriage of promotion, visibility, quality, efficiency and litigation. The concept of trimming costs, increasing visibility, i.e. sales and accomplishing those goals within legal boundaries basically defined the business protocol in general. The Wallrath protocol followed a much more defined path. Dick and Patsy almost lived within a world of their own because they understood the foundations of the Twelve Step Program and the reasons those fundamental principles were indoctrinated to the window company. Dick fired many employees for simply lying to customers, to their supervisors or to their peers. Employees were fired for lying to cover for other employees. The company bills were paid by the tenth, the staff was expected to show up for work on time and give an honest day's work and the management team was held to the same standards.

As the company grew and success followed, the leeches came out of the woodwork. Patsy was often times the buffer between Dick and the clouded facts surrounding a request for assistance. Patsy was the comptroller for the company, Dick's wife briefly and Dick's partner for life. If someone did not want Dick Wallrath to know a particular fact or detail, they did not share that particular detail with Patsy Murphy. The distant relatives, acquaintances and long lost pals came calling quicker than Red Rock threw each bull rider that climbed up aboard his big-ass back. Patsy helped present the facts in each request for Dick's assistance. In the end, the final call was Dick's alone. Patsy did not always agree with the decisions that Dick made, but she respected those decisions for what they were. It may have been the early failures, a genetic function or a gratitude mechanism for his own transformation, but Patsy witnessed the generosity that would define Dick's life from a rare perspective. There were few regrets and the underlying motivation behind the benevolence was not calculated, but simply Dick's desire to give back something. God gave Dick the tools to work with. He rarely wasted the knowledge.

Patsy Murphy: I can recall the early days of the window company, when we needed a new piece of equipment. Manufacturing of any kind is an exercise in cost management and the easiest way to pace any company out of any market is to fall behind the technology of the industry. At Champion, we were acutely aware of those needs. As with many companies, when new equipment is needed, the money to purchase that new equipment is not always available. There were times when Champion needed an extension of credit for the purpose of fulfilling our obligations to our suppliers. During all those times, Dick insisted on giving twenty percent of our revenues to charity. I used to throw a fit! I would ask Dick, how can we give money away that we do not have? I wrote the checks! I knew what we owed. I told Dick on many occasions that we do not have the money to continue the charitable contributions. Hell, I told him that we could pick it up when we had a better cash flow. We could even double up to make up for the down time, but we had to stop giving money away that we did not have. Dick refused to alter his plan. Remember the plan that was inspired by Robert Gilmore LeTourneau. Mr. Le Tourneau gave twenty percent of whatever he took in to charity. After that, he was confident to let the chips fall wherever. Dick felt that he had to forge his path under those guidelines and a Southern Pacific Railroad twin-diesel engine was not going to knock him off the track. Dick made a pact with God and bankruptcy was a far easier failure than the alternative. My admiration for Dick Wallrath grew tremendously. His actions defined my growth and I will always be grateful for the example of Dick's resolve. My relationship with Dick has certainly defined my own maturation and growth.

The relationship between Dick Wallrath and Patsy Murphy has been a journey that is far from over and remains an exciting dance today. Many marriages have track records that have lead couples into the abyss of complacency. Too many couples play the second-guessing game of what ifs. "What if I had met someone else?" "What if I had finished school and put off children?" "What if I had followed my own dreams, rather than his dreams?" Individuals grow and change immeasurably over the course of three decades. Would there be a marriage or even a connection if the same two people met twenty years later? Would those two people find each other as the individuals that they have become? There are many questions as to the compatibility of couples after living together for so many years. How does twenty or thirty years alter a couple? Is it fair to expect each person in a marriage to evolve in tandem? Most often the answer is no. Dick and Patsy have grown together as the years have advanced. Their shared experience of turning their lives over to a power greater than their own has remained an infinite bond between them.

Patsy Murphy: Dick has owned a series of ranches in Texas over the years. He has always loved to spend time away from the city and we eventually moved to Centerville on a full-time basis some years ago. Each year, Dick would pick a church or a particular preacher that resided in or around the county where the ranch Dick owned was located. The selection was always made prior to the holidays of Thanksgiving and Christmas. Dick would purchase a tremendous amount of food for the particular parish, church or preacher. I would deliver the food a few days before the holiday in question. The food was intended to give families without much food a special holiday meal. The selection and distribution of the meals was up to the individual church or preacher. My instructions were always very simple. I was to deliver the food and simply say that they were a gift from God. In a way, they were.

CHAPTER 8

Chapter Eight...Vanessa Smith

April 8, 2005

Dear Mr. Pomerantz,

I am writing to you in response to the news about a book being written about Mr. Wallrath. I am one of the many youths across the state who have benefited from participating in stock shows. I am not quite certain that you need my letter or how the letter might be used, but I want to write to you about Mr. Wallrath and you can use the letter however you chose.

I was involved with 4-H for ten years. I started in the third grade with two very simple projects. I had a livestock project, which consisted of raising two sheep. They were named Salt and Pepper, pretty original? I also made a dress, which I entered into a 4-H fashion show. At the county stock show that year, I received a first and a second place for my two lambs. I did not participate in any major stock shows that year, but I could not wait to get started for the next season. Those modest beginnings got me to where I am today. My involvement in 4-H from an early age has taught me about responsibility, confidence, leadership, honor, integrity and determination. I truly do feel like my affiliation with 4-H has given me a foothold to achieve my goals. Without the 4-H affiliation, I am not certain how I would have turned out. I strongly doubt that I would have the same ideals and the same determination to move forward. The experiences gained through my work in 4-H have been invaluable to my life as a college freshman at Texas A & M University. It is clearly evident that other students have not been as well prepared as I have been. 4-H has given me the tools to be strong, opinionated and not afraid to pursue my dreams.

Not only was my lamb project my main 4-H project, but it was a project that the entire family could participate. Many families have difficulty relating to each other, whether it is the children relating to their parents or vice versa. Many parents and teenagers have

113

trouble with even the simplest form of communication. My 4-H project was something my father and I could always talk about. I loved going to the barn with him. It will remain one of my fondest memories. I am certain that those special times with my dad brought us closer together. Traveling to the many stock shows was a family affair. My mom, dad and I would go together. We spent time in the hotels, on the road, back and forth to the stock show arenas and we all shared in the care of the animals. The length of time for each show varied, depending on well we did. If we showed well, then we got to hang around until the end of the week. The bond between our family grew very strong over the years and the stock shows were a big part of the time we got to spend together.

Early in my 4-H career, my dad was learning the ropes with me. It took us awhile to be able to spot the good sheep, so we stumbled a bit before we were able to place and win consistently. I remember getting my first dot at a major stock show. (A dot is where you make it to the sale and they place a dot on the shoulder of the lamb to mark him.) The show was the San Antonio Stock Show. I was in junior high school at the time. I received second place for one of my sheep. By the time I got to high school, I had placed at every major stock show in Texas except the Houston Stock Show. That was the one that I coveted. I had been very close in previous years, but that prestigious red dot kept eluding me. It was not until my sophomore year in high school that I was able to place at the Houston Stock Show. I received a fifth place for one of my sheep. I placed in Houston every year after that until my graduation from high school.

The experiences that I had during those stock shows are times that I will never forget. I plan on staying involved with 4-H for my entire life. I know my own family will benefit from the 4-H experience just as I have. As I said before, I currently attend Texas A & M

University and I could not imagine myself at any other university. I love going to school here and I seriously doubt that without the help from men like Mr. Wallrath and organizations like 4-H, that I would be here at all. I credit 4-H with much of what I have in life and I will credit the same organization for much of what I have in the future. The question of where I would have been without 4-H is a question that I do not have to address. The reality today is that the cost of a college education is rising faster than most families can adjust to. My family, like so many others, is an average income family that has worked very hard to sustain all of us at that level. Our income is too high to qualify for any substantial aid in college tuition and too small to be able to afford the total cost of college. I have been able to supplement my tuition with some scholarship money and a variety of parent and student loans. The scholarship money is from the Houston Livestock Show and Rodeo Scholarship Fund. I received the scholarship through the 4-H Opportunity Scholarship. Mr. Wallrath is my contact for the organization because the money that I have received came from the fund that was set up as a memorial fund for Mr. Wallrath's daughter, Dina. I am extremely grateful for the scholarship money that I have received. It will not cover the entire cost of college, but without that help, I may not be where I am today. Thank you again to Mr. Wallrath and 4-H for the help you have provided.

Vanessa Smith

July 20, 2004

In Memory of Dina Wallrath Robertson by Champion Windows

To: Richard Wallrath

Centerville, Texas

Dear Mr. Wallrath,

I would like to thank you for the generous contributions that you have made to the Houston Livestock Show and Rodeo Scholarship Fund. I would also like to apologize for the tardiness of my letter. The first letter that I sent to you was returned last Monday because I had the wrong address on it. If you have any questions regarding the deadline for thank you notes that I missed, please contact the 4-H Foundation Office. I made certain that they knew that my error was the only reason my note was late and I apologized to them for the delay in my recognition of your generosity.

I am very thankful for selfless act that you have done in order to help students achieve their goals. I am a 4-H Scholar and I am a 2004 recipient of this scholarship. The commitment that you have made each year to support the youth of Texas is one that we all recognize and appreciate. I, personally, am very grateful for the contributions that you have given to me in order to facilitate my educational career. I will be working hard for the next few years to justify the contributions made by everyone.

I will be attending Texas A & M University in the fall and will be majoring in Agribusiness. I have already been to orientation and have registered for my fall classes. You will soon be receiving in the mail, my official course schedule. I am looking forward to experiencing the campus life and learning about the traditions that I am about to take part in.

Thank you again for your continued support over the years. It is greatly appreciated and I am looking forward to staying in touch with you.

Thank You,

Vanessa Smith

CHAPTER 9

Chapter Nine...Houston and San Antonio, High Stakes Steers

Introduction...

The Houston Livestock Show and Rodeo & The San Antonio Stock Show and Rodeo

The Houston Livestock Show and Rodeo and The San Antonio Stock Show and Rodeo are charities, 501 c (3) organizations, that benefit the youth of Texas. Since 1957, The Houston Livestock Show and Rodeo has raised a total educational commitment of more than $100 million. In the fall of 2003, there were nearly 2,000 students enrolled at almost 100 Texas colleges and universities on direct scholarships from the Houston Livestock Show and Rodeo. Since 1950, The San Antonio Stock Show and Rodeo has raised more than $58 million with a record $6.1 million committed in 2004. The money is used for a variety of efforts including scholarships, grants, endowments, auctions, calf scramble programs and show premiums paid to youth participants.

For example, in 2005 at the Houston Livestock Show and Rodeo, a total of 1,740,095 visitors in general attendance, were counted for all activities on the grounds at Reliant Stadium and the adjacent facilities. Rodeo attendance topped 1.1 million and the concert attendance rose almost identical to the rodeo attendance at well over 1.1 million concert goers. Alicia Keys, Kenny Chesney and Hillary Duff headlined the stadium. Martina McBride, Pat Green and many others continued to pack 'em in. The Grand Champion Steer went for $340,000. The total junior auction sales totaled $6,823,219. The San Antonio line-up of Alan Jackson, Brooks and Dunn, Willie Nelson, Dierks Bentley, Bill Cosby, Rascal Flatts, Clay Walker and Reba McEntire kept the attendance levels at record pace. The live-stock show in Houston boasted 31,720 entries and 1738 international guests from 52 countries.

All applicants for Houston Livestock Show scholarships must meet the following requirements.

1) They must be a United States citizen.

2) They must attend a public high school from which they will graduate at mid-term or in the spring of the year in which they seek an award.

3) They must be a resident of the state of Texas.

4) They must attend a Texas college or university and have applied for admission to such an institution.

5) They must meet academic standards for class rank and SAT/ACT scores as stated in the application.

The stock shows offer scholarship awards to the Future Farmers of America (FFA), 4-H Clubs and Family Career and Community Leaders of Amerca (FCCLA). The entry exhibitors:

1) Must be eight years old and in the third grade but not more than nineteen years old by February 1 of the current year.

2) Must be enrolled in a Texas 4-H Club or a Texas FFA Chapter for this particular project and be under the supervision of a County Agent or Teacher of Vocational Agriculture.

3) Must not have completed their high school education.

In layman's terms, the young people enter a steer (there are many other animal entries at the stock shows, but for this book we are describing the steer auctions) that they have raised from sometime after the young bovine (scientific name for cattle) is born. Most young people begin raising their young steers when the animal is five to six months old. The youth groups with their agriculture teachers will visit large cattle operations in Texas and purchase young steers. The kids raise the young steer for approximately eleven to eighteen months. Ring steers are usually between eighteen and twenty months old. The steers are shaved before most stock shows to eliminate the ability to hide any imperfections on the animals. Animals are judged on size with relation to the breed, marked muscle distribution, fat content, disposition, color and presence. Are the steers lethargic? Do they show energy? How do the kids handle the animals? Does it appear that they have been the primary source of care or does it appear that an adult or substitute has done much of the work? Is the animal skittish with the youngster? There are more than 2,500 steers of sixteen different breeds entered into a show like Houston. The breeds are:

Charolais, Limousin, Shorthorn, Crossbreds, Angus, Hereford, Brangus, Brahman, Chianina, Maine-Anjou, Santa Gertrudis, Simmental, Red Angus, Polled Hereford, American Breeds/Crossbreeds

The animals are judged and each breed will have produced a Grand Champion and Reserve Champion. Among the sixteen Grand Champions and sixteen reserve Champions, an overall Grand Champion and overall Reserve Champion will be selected. The money raised at the auctions is directly donated to the scholarship programs. Payments are guaranteed to each placing steer. The "Bonus Pool" funds are used to offset any lots that did not sell for the guaranteed payment and for auction expenses. Any Bonus Pool funds remaining after all guaranteed payments have been met and all auction expenses have been satisfied, are shared among the placing exhibitors. No exhibitor shall receive more than the Potential Maximum Payment. Guaranteed payment awards are as follows:

Grand Champion $75,000

Reserve Grand Champion $40,000

Breed Champion Steers $15,000

Reserve Breed Champion Steers $12,500

Remaining First Place Steers $6,000

Remaining Second Place Steers $5,000

Remaining Third Place steers $3,000

Remaining Fourth Place Steers $2,750

Remaining Fifth Place Steers $2,500

All Remaining Placing Steers $2,000

The money awarded goes directly to the young person involved with raising and showing the steer. The steers are sold at auction and slaughtered a few days later. The auction buyer will receive the hide for an additional premium. Meat packages are offered to all buyers, but rarely come from the purchased steer. The buyer does not have the option to save the steer and return it to the youngster.

Dick Wallrath has been actively purchasing steers from the Houston Livestock Show and Rodeo and the San Antonio Stock Show and Rodeo for the past seven years. To date, Dick Wallrath has purchased steers totaling $3.5 million at Houston and $1 million at San Antonio. Dick has purchased numerous Grand Champions, topping out with Popcorn in Houston for $600,001 in 2002. Dick has spent over one-half million dollars in Austin on stock show steers. During the past twenty-four months, Dick Wallrath has donated one million dollars directly to FFA and one million dollars directly to 4-H Clubs. Dick Wallrath has established an endowment scholarship fund program that will be distributed from FFA and 4-H. The endowment is solely funded by Mr. Wallrath and structured to pay out a growing number of scholarships for decades to come. Mr. Wallrath has immediate plans for additional millions to be donated under the watchful eyes of the newly organized awards program.

What the Hell is a Livestock Show?

The concept of a stock show to most Americans has to be an event associated with a NASCAR race. Stock cars and stock shows must be related? A swine auction would certainly conjure up some contorted facial expressions and the tilted puppy dog look of a quizzical lost soul. While the rodeo competition attracts the majority of the mainstream media, the stock shows associated with the major rodeos have raised millions of dollars for scholarships programs across the West. From the boardrooms in Manhattan to the trading pits of the Chicago Board of Trade, from the conference tables at General Motors to the Teamster Union Bargaining tables, the image of successful men and women bidding tremendous sums of money for a pig or a steer is not explicable. Here are the guidelines. Apparently sane men and women spend more than one-half million dollars on a single castrated bull on Saturday. Their prized purchase is a shaved two thousand-pound steer and for the investment, the animal is slaughtered on Monday. The carcass is carved up for a meat package (not necessarily their own) and some steroid tissue samples. The buyers, not only, do not get the meat from the animal they purchased, they are required to spend an additional five-thousand dollars to obtain the hide from the same animal they purchased during the auction.

Let's review the sequence of events that highlight the steer auctions of the largest livestock auctions in the world. First, attend the auction as a VIP buyer. Second, spend upwards of $500,000 to purchase the event Grand Champion or $250,000 to purchase the event Reserve Grand Champion. Third, say good-bye to your newly purchased steer because he has two more days to smell the roses, then he is carved up and sent to the nearest Burger King processing plant. Fourth, have your photograph taken with some local and state politicians, the animal you purchased and the child responsible for raising that animal. Fifth, write your six-figure check and wave bye-bye to the unsuspecting, newly crowned Grand Champion.

Only now, do we fully begin to comprehend why many American citizens still believe that Texas could function as a nation alone. Wealthy people need to throw six figures at a glorified Big Mac like ranchers in Texas need a Sherpa guide and an altimeter. Dick Wallrath was happy building his window company business and contributing regularly to the local chapters of the Shriner organizations. Dick always had a soft spot in his heart for children and made certain that Champion Window Company always purchased more than its' share of circus tickets and hospital raffle chances. In 1990, the game changed. Pat and Andy Vavra invited Dick Wallrath and Patsy Murphy to their first big time rodeo. Pat Vavra's father had been very involved with quarter horses and his box seats to the Houston Livestock Show and Rodeo were instrumental in Dick's first visit to a livestock auction.

Patsy Murphy: In 1991, Dick and Andy decided to attend the lamb auction at the Houston Livestock Show and Rodeo. Dick had to receive a buyer's number to participate in the auction. His number was "911". On that first visit, the sight of those little kids struggling to get the animals under control got to Dick. The boys and girls were required to lead their animals across the show pit for the buyers to observe and bid on their projects. Dick bought a couple lambs on his first visit to the auctions. After that first auction, Dick began to research every aspect of the live auctions. He was particularly interested in how much of the money that was raised at each auction went directly to the children and their scholarship needs. Dick had been very active in other charitable causes, including the Boys and

Girls Country of Hockley, Texas. Dick had helped to build multiple houses under the tutelage of the Boys and Girls Country. The religious emphasis and direction of some organizations eventually failed to meet Dick's criteria of simply having no hidden agendas that superceded providing assistance to those less fortunate. Dick did not attempt to invoke any personal ideologies upon any organization and subsequently felt these same organizations had to practice a similar policy for his continued involvement. The livestock shows proved to be just such an avenue.

As mentioned earlier, The Houston Livestock Show and Rodeo is a 501 © (3) charitable event. The operating budget for the Livestock Show and Rodeo has always been raised by the proceeds from the rodeo itself, the carnival, the concerts and the concession dollars. The money raised from the auctions themselves went directly to the children and the scholarship fund. When Dick discovered the focused direction of the stock shows, he challenged Andy to get on the Steer Auction Committee at the Houston Stock Show and Rodeo. Andy was first selected to be on the lamb auction committee. That same year, as a rookie, Andy was selected to be on the steer auction committee. These were influential appointments and the access to information for the steer auction committee members was crucial to Dick Wallrath's comfort level and further involvement.

At the 2005 Houston Livestock Show and Rodeo, Junior Auction sales totaled an unofficial $6,823,219. The importance of that money actually landing in the scholarship fund for Texas youth and not hidden as operating expenses for the auction itself was the first priority for Dick Wallrath. On the evening of May 24, 2005, the Houston Livestock Show and Rodeo put on display the pot of gold that so many HLSR volunteer workers contributed to each year. The HLSR awards presentation doled out nearly four million dollars in college scholarships to area youth. Three scholarship programs, Metropolitan, Opportunity and School Art, brought 312 outstanding area students together on the floor of Reliant Stadium. Each student received a scholarship worth $12,000. The general scholarship fund for a myriad of youth organizations continued to grow with each successful auction.

Again, we go back to the auction boundaries. The steer auctions worked on a sliding scale of proceeds. There were sixteen breeds with three different weight classes in each breed. The heavyweight class within each breed was the most visible. Each separate breed had a Grand Champion and a Reserve Grand Champion selected. From those sixteen Grand Champions and sixteen Reserve Grand Champions, a show Grand Champion and show Reserve Grand Champion were selected. The money raised for each steer was distributed according to the chart on page 122 of this book. The dollars fell off quickly after the Champion and Reserve Champion levels. Dick's early research into the stock shows and the real dollars awarded to the children left some holes in the process according to Mr. Wallrath's math. As a businessman, if one had to spend fifteen hundred dollars to raise and show an animal, a fifteen hundred-dollar reward was a wash. Dick decided that his early mission would be to raise those middle awards out of the break even or loss category and give those kids something to put in the bank.

Andy Vavra: Dick was a foreigner to his first lamb auction. I think Dick spent nearly $17,000 at that first lamb auction. That was in the early to mid-nineties. I had only one thought at the time and that was admiration for Dick's generosity. I had no clue that over the next dozen years, Dick Wallrath would purchase more premium steers than any other buyer in the history of the Houston Livestock Show and Rodeo. After Dick's first lamb auction purchases, we attended the steer auction held on the next morning. Dick insisted on a good seat, so the auctioneer could see him front and center. Dick told me to keep track of what he was spending. He was given a number by his accountant and was told that number was to be the maximum contribution to be spent at the auction. Dick wanted to be aware of the dollars, but the instructions from his accountant had no bearing on his intentions. The money raised at most stock shows fell off dramatically from the Grand Champion to the Reserve Grand Champion. The money evaporated even faster after the Reserve Grand Champion was purchased. Dick was most concerned about the middle and lower rounds of the steer auction. The money raised was barely enough to cover the expenses of raising the steer for an entire year or more. What the hell was the purpose of the auction if the Gosh darn buyers couldn't even pony up for the cost to get there. Dick jumped all over the middle rounds during that first and second year. In Dick's second visit to the HLSR, Dick spent close to $80,000 on twelve steers. The Houston Livestock Show and Rodeo had been put on notice.

The history of livestock shows and the buyers that have attended those shows were a history of tradition. The mission was always in the right place, but the traditional methods left a clogged tunnel to jack up the awards. In San Antonio, the Grand Champion had always been purchased by a rotation of three or four buying groups. The willingness of those groups to step up to the table year after year, in down economies and in good years, proved to be nothing short of relentless generosity. The awards, however, grew slowly and by design. If the Grand Champion in San Antonio sold one year for $50,000 to one group, then the next year, the price would be pre-arranged to peak at or near $51,000. The Grand Champion purchase would then be awarded to the next group in the rotation. In 1995, the Grand Champion Steer was purchased by the group of Rush Enterprises, (tractor-trailers), HEB Grocery and Miller Beer Company for the price of $66,000. The same group with the addition of a funeral home sponsor purchased the Grand Champion Steer in 1996 for $67,500.

The purchase of the Grand Champion at a major livestock show and rodeo was extremely prestigious. There were often picture sessions with the Governor and other political figures attending. There were publicity photos in the major newspapers. There were colorful championship banners and hand-tooled gold buckles for the championship buyers. There were parades into the main arena for the next evenings' rodeo performances. The parades were accompanied by individual introductions to a packed stadium of the Grand Champion and Reserve Grand Champion steers, owners and their buyers. The purchase of any Grand Champion was followed by some well-deserved, serious ass kissing. Dick wanted the focus placed on the dollar awards given to the children.

Andy Vavra: I remember when Dick and I went to San Antonio in 1997. I'm not certain if Dick had been there before, but I know that he was not a player in their livestock sale circles. The San Antonio Grand Champion rotation was fairly well known, but Dick came into town with other ideas. During that first year, the bidding for the Grand Champion held to form for the initial phase of the sale. The four groups involved pushed the dollars up to roughly $50,000. After the $50,000 level had been reached, the leaps got smaller and the bids dwindled accordingly. The rotation would land at the pre-arranged price and the chosen group would claim the Grand Champion. Dick Wallrath threw a monkey wrench

into the festivities. Dick entered the bidding as the bids were supposed to stop. He leaped

over the unexpected group rotation and purchased the Grand Champion for $69,000 before

the groups could huddle and devise a strategy to oust the new guy from Houston. The cus-

tomary group rotation was stunned. The money raised for the kids had been greatly

increased and the benefit outweighed any petty squabbles about who bought what, but this

was Texas, where pride and common sense often took different trains. The groups snapped

into action when the Reserve Grand Champion came up for bid. Dick entered the fray right

away. The other groups were determined to keep Dick from buying the Reserve Grand

Champion as well. They jacked the bidding up at a rapid pace. Dick pulled out of the bid-

ding quietly. The result was paralytic. The Reserve Grand Champion in 1997 at San

Antonio sold for $70,000, an unheard of proposition that placed the money for the Reserve

Grand Champion at more than the Grand Champion. In keeping Dick Wallrath from buy-

ing the Reserve Grand Champion, Rush Enterprises made stock show history. Dick

Wallrath succeeded on two fronts. First, Mr. Wallrath's bidding tactics pushed the awards

up substantially. Secondly, the unwritten rules were now changed and the standard rotation

had to rethink their approach.

In 1998, Dick Wallrath purchased the Grand Champion in San Antonio and had decid-

ed to attempt to push up the Reserve Grand Champion's price as he did the year before.

There had to be the same resentment for his style, especially after he had grabbed the

Grand Champion two years in a row. The buying groups in San Antonio had done some

homework and they hung the Reserve Grand Champion on Dick that year, when he did not have the initial plan to buy both champions. The end result was perfectly plausible for Dick Wallrath. He always left San Antonio with a smile. He left a few smiles along the way as well. Dick's record at San Antonio has been as follows:

1) 1997-Champion Window Company and Dick Wallrath purchased the Grand Champion for $69,000.

2) 1998-Champion Window Company and Dick Wallrath purchased the Grand Champion for $75,000 and the Reserve Grand Champion for $47,500.

3) 1999-Champion Window Company and Dick Wallrath purchased seven breed champions for a total of $80,000.

4) 2000-Champion Window Company and Dick Wallrath purchased nine breed champions for a total of $106,000.

5) 2001-Champion Window Company and Dick Wallrath purchased the Grand Champion for $87,000 and five breed champions for a total of $133,500.

6) 2002-Champion Window Company and Dick Wallrath purchased the Reserve Grand Champion and ten breed champions for a total of $110,000.

7) 2003-Champion Window Company and Dick Wallrath purchased ten breed champions for a total of $90,500.

8) 2004-Champion Window Company and Dick Wallrath purchased nine breed champions for a total of $95,000.

9) 2005-Champion Window Company and Dick Wallrath purchased eleven breed champion and two reserve breed champions for a total of $122,500.

Dick Wallrath has amassed a total of $929,000 in steer purchases from the San Antonio Stock Show and Rodeo over the past nine years.

The stock shows have grown in the state of Texas to unimagined levels of participation and compensation. In 2005, the steer auction judges had to examine more than 2200 steers. The judges generally come out of the heartland of America. The judges are never from the state of Texas. Most come from educational backgrounds such as professors from schools like the University of Kansas or the University of Nebraska. All judges have an extensive background in the cattle business and/or a comprehensive agricultural expertise focused on feedlots, meatpacking or ranch management in general. Blood and urine samples are taken from the animals during the first inspection. A positive test for steroids will mandate an automatic expulsion from the competition. The Grand Champion and Reserve Grand Champion of each breed are selected on Friday morning before the Saturday sale. On Friday night, the overall show Grand Champion and Reserve Grand Champion are selected. There are 428 money-producing positions in the stock sale. The first 108 qualify for the carcass contest. If a buyer spends more than $5,000 for a steer, then that buyer is entitled to purchase the hide for an additional fee. The first 108 steers sold are slaughtered on Monday after the Saturday sale. Once the animal is slaughtered, tissue samples from the eyes, tongue, brain and liver are tested for illegal growth additives or steroids. Enhancing agents show more prevalent in these tissue samples. The hides are shipped to Mexico where they are tanned and sent back to the buyer.

The buyers do not have the option to save the animal. Dick has been involved with more than one steer purchase where the child who raised the animal was devastated after the sale. The child was crying and Dick inquired about simply giving the animal back to the child as opposed to slaughtering the steer. The requests were denied. The function of the program is to raise money for scholarships through the skills development of raising cattle for beef production only. A feel-good family movie about livestock auctions was shot in 2001 called "Grand Champion." The movie was about a boy who refused to give up his Grand Champion steer to the slaughterhouse. After the sale, the steer and the boy who raised the steer, disappeared. The movie featured Tie Down World Champion Joe Beaver's son, Brody, and a host of Texas rodeo and entertainment legends. The list included George Strait, Larry Mayan, Roy Cooper, Tuff Hedeman, Bruce Willis and Julia Roberts.

While the judging circles have been squeaky clean over the years, an occasional hiccup has occurred within the tissue testing requirements. A positive tissue test will produce an automatic disqualification and a forfeiture of the scholarship money that had been award-ed. In the late eighties, the oil fire fighter, Red Adair purchased a Grand Champion steer in Houston. After the slaughter, the steer tested positive for growth hormones. The schol-arship money was revoked and the Reserve Grand Champion was moved up.

Through the years at the Houston Livestock Show and Rodeo, Dick had amassed a rep-utation for running up the middle bids and greatly increasing the money each child got to take home from his or her show animal. Since Dick Wallrath began his journeys to the Houston Stock Show and Rodeo, Dick has purchased steers in excess of $3.5 million. Among the highlights:

1) 2002-Dick Wallrath paid one-half of the winning bid on the HLSR (Houston Livestock Show and Rodeo) Grand Champion. The bid was $600,001, a record for one steer sold at auction in the United States.

2) 2003-Dick Wallrath purchased the HLSR Grand Champion for $350,000.

3) 2004-Dick Wallrath purchased the HLSR Grand Champion for $250,000.

The slogan for Cheyenne Days is "The Grandaddy of Them All!" The Houston

Livestock Show and Rodeo could claim the moniker of simply "The Show" or "The Broadway Stage of Livestock Shows". The Houston Livestock Show and Rodeo has been responsible for among other projects, a sixty million dollar renovation of the Astrodome and a few years later, a one-third partnership in the financing, construction and operation of Reliant Stadium. In conjunction with the Houston Texans and the taxpayers, the HLSR has been front and center in the development of one of the nation's most complete stadium complexes.

The "Grandaddy" purchase of them all was in 2002. The previous record purchase for a Grand Champion steer had been $600,000 by a group that included internationally known World Wrestling Champion "Stone Cold" Steve Austin. In 2002, Dick Wallrath and partner Virgil Wagner had determined that they would share the cost of the Grand Champion and seek the record. The record was reached at $600,001. Dick and Virgil had previously arranged to share equally in the cost and the publicity associated with a Grand Champion purchase. The publicity is good for the business of steer auctions and the business of continued corporate support for the scholarship programs. When the time came in 2002 to take pictures with the Grand Champion steer, Virgil Wagner hauled up another couple to the podium and informed Mr. Wallrath that his contribution would be shared by the new couple. They all shared equally in the photo session and they rode together in the Grand Entry during the evening rodeo performance. Mr. Wallrath paid $300,000 and the remaining partners each paid $150,000. Equal partners had a funny ring to it.

On the morning of the steer auction in Houston, a breakfast is held every year for the steer auction buyers and their guests. It was March 12, 2005. The breakfast was held at Reliant Arena. The guest list included more than nineteen hundred buyers and guests. The security staff and committee members brought the total to well over two thousand. The steer auction was held at noon at an adjacent structure called the Reliant Arena Sales Pavilion. The breakfast was an annual function that served to thank the buyers for their continued support and traditionally jump-started the bidding wars by fueling the spending tanks of those in attendance. At the 2005 breakfast, the featured speakers were Texas Republican Senator Kay Bailey Hutchison and Texas Governor Rick Perry.

Senator Hutchison won a third term to the United States Senate in 2004. Senator Hutchison grew up in La Marque, Texas and graduated from the University of Texas and UT Law School. She was twice elected to the Texas House of Representatives and also served as Texas State Treasurer. She has been Vice-Chairman of the Senate Republican Conference and was the fifth-highest ranking Republican Senator. Senator Hutchison has been the Chairman of the Military Construction and Veterans Affairs Subcommittee, a member of the Defense Subcommittee of the Senate Appropriations Committee and has played a key role in shaping America's defense policies during such volatile times. Speculation at the time of the 2005 HLSR had the Senator returning to Texas in 2006 and seeking the Republican nomination for Governor against the man she would be sharing the 2005 HLSR breakfast podium with. (Since the 2005 HLSR, Senator Hutchison has decided not to seek the 2006 Gubernatorial nomination in Texas.) Senator Hutchison spoke first. Her address was poignant and funny. The object of the breakfast was not to instigate a political debate, but to thank those attending for their support and encourage the open wallets to reach deeper than ever during the upcoming steer auction. The Senator spoke highly of Governor Perry and thanked the crowd for inviting her to such a special occasion for Texans.

Dick Wallrath had the privilege to introduce the Governor of Texas. Governor Perry and Mr. Wallrath had gained a mutual respect and genuine friendship for each other over the years. Their friendship grew from a shared commitment to the youth of Texas. Rick Perry, the 47th governor of Texas, had served nearly two decades in public service since graduating from Texas A & M University and serving four and a half years in the United States Air Force. The Governor and Mr. Wallrath embraced as Rick Perry took the stage. The Texas native, originally from Paint Creek, north of Abilene, returned the kind words from the Texas Senator.

Governor Perry began his address by reviewing the accomplishments of HLSR and singling out the generosity of Dick Wallrath. The Governor focused on the importance of all the work accomplished by the hard-working staff of HLSR. Their tireless efforts helped to raise the hopes and dreams of countless Texas young people. Mr. Tom Davis, Chairman of the Steer Auction Committee at HLSR, stepped forward with a challenge for the Governor. Mr. Davis related a conversation he had with his daughter, the night before the HLSR breakfast. His daughter had complained about the light tips generated by the student population at Texas A & M University. Tom Davis joined the Governor at the podium for the story. Mr. Davis then explained to the crowd that his daughter had taken a job as a waitress during the school year. Tom Davis had an idea that could help his daughter. Mr. Davis bet his daughter two weeks worth of tips that the Governor would never stand up at the Steer Auction Breakfast and give the "Hook-Em Horns" sign for the nineteen hundred guests in attendance. Governor Perry stood contemplating the story in typical Texas style. He rubbed his hand slowly across his mouth to emphasize each phase of the offer. Governor Perry was wearing blue jeans, a white Oxford shirt minus the tie, traditional cowboy boots and a dark blue Polo jacket. The jacket collar was flipped up in typical Ralph Lauren mode. Former World Champion Bull Rider Bobby Steiner and Governor Perry had arrived on the Governors jet from Austin just minutes before the breakfast began.

The request was, as they say, looming large. First, it would be sacrilegious for a Texas A & M graduate to give the University of Texas, "hook 'em horns" sign. Tom Davis' daughter was certain that the Governor would help her out and hold up the Longhorn symbol. The sacrifice would lighten the load for Tom's daughter. The governor relayed his dilemma to the audience. After some quiet thought and some chin scratching, the Texas Governor had made up his mind. He pointed to Tom Davis.

"As much as I love all children and would do most anything to make life better for them," the Governor began, "I am afraid that your daughter is just going to have to pick up a few more shifts. There is no way I am going to stand up here and give the "hook 'em horns" sign for a measly two weeks of tips at a college café." The large audience laughed as the Governor shrugged his shoulders like there was nothing he could do. The Governor then raised his hand to quiet the crowd and proposed another alternative.

"I will, after some careful thought, consider one alternative." The Governor announced. "If the distinguished Senator from Texas would join me on the stage, I have another proposal." Governor Perry looked over at Senator Kay Bailey Hutchison. "I will stand up here one time and one time only and give the "hook 'em horns" sign. I will give this symbol only if the Senator will stand next to me and give the "gig 'em Aggies" thumbs up sign. This is as big a sin for a Longhorn as it is for an Aggie to consider what I am considering." The audience roared their approval.

"The only catch," Governor Perry continued, "To this once in a lifetime event is that one of you buyers has to tack on an additional $50,000 to the price paid for the Grand Champion Steer coming up here in about thirty minutes. You have about two minutes to ante up or this offer is off the table." The Governor smiled as the Senator joined him at the podium.

"One minute." The Governor reminded the buyers. A slew of hands shot up from the audience. Governor Perry shook his head and rolled his eyes. Senator Hutchison laughed out loud.

"Get the names down." Governor Perry ordered as he pointed to the raised hands in the audience. He took the Senator's hand and they walked down to the floor in front of the podium.

"Get the cameras up here. This is only going to happen briefly and then never again." The Governor looked up and waved off the first cameras. "No, no, no." Perry announced. "I want the big cameras up here. Go get the television cameras. I don't want those dinky little hand held jobs."

The cameras were set in place. The audience was silent in anticipation. The Governor and the Senator each raised their arms. The opposing salutes were extended. The cameras converged closer. The audience flashed hundreds of personal cameras. Governor Perry and Senator Hutchison shook hands and the breakfast came to a close. The entire group walked to the Reliant Sales Pavilion. The steer auction kicked off at noon and set another record for auction totals when the last animal was sold. Governor Perry posed for pictures with the Grand Champion buyers. The winning bid on the Grand Champion for 2005 was $340,000, plus another $50,000.

Champion Windows Scholarship

Mr. Dick Wallrath

In Memory of Dina Wallrath Robertson

Presented through

Houston Livestock Show and Rodeo

The partnership between the Houston Livestock Show and Rodeo and the Texas 4-H Youth Development Foundation began in 1954 and has contributed greatly to the education of the youth of the State of Texas. When the Houston Livestock Show and Rodeo presented its first educational scholarship in the amount of $4,000 a wonderful tradition was established into what would become a major multi-million dollar educational program supporting Texas young people. Now, more than forty years later, Houston's mission is still defined by the thousands of youth, who annually receive financial support. Each year, the Show provides through the Texas 4-H Youth Development Foundation seventy $10,000 scholarships statewide from proceeds from the livestock auctions. The successful auctions are made possible through the generous contributions of many individuals and corporations.

The owner of Champion Windows, a Houston based firm, is one of those individuals. Among his many contributions, Mr. Dick Wallrath has provided numerous scholarships of $10,000 each in memory of his daughter, Dina Wallrath Robertson and numerous scholarships of $10,000 each from Champion Windows. Mr. Wallrath has used his own personal resources and the resources of his company to fund the educational programs targeted by the Houston Livestock Show and Rodeo. Mr. Wallrath's contributions to the Texas 4-H and Texas Youth Scholarship Programs has reached far beyond that of simply

139

supporting the cause. The goals of Texas 4-H Opportunity Scholarship Programs are to make as many scholarships available to Texas young people to attend the Texas colleges or universities of their choice and to pursue a broad range of academic majors. Mr. Wallrath has made a tremendous impact in those scholarship numbers.

CHAPTER 10

Chapter Ten... Emilie Hartfield

Emilie's 2003 4-H Opportunity Scholarship Application...from the

Personal Narrative section.

"Emilie, it is time to go to Kindergarten." My mom would say. "Aren't you excited to

meet new friends and learn new things?"

"Mom, I don't need to go to Kindergarten. I already learned everything last year in pre-

school." Came my now famous reply to my mother when I first started school twelve years

ago. Boy, was I wrong. There were so many adventures just waiting for me.

My name is Emilie Hartfield and I am an active teenager. Since that first day of

Kindergarten long ago, I have been involved in nearly every single extracurricular activi-

ty that my schools offered. I was involved with 4-H, FFA, basketball, track, softball,

Fellowship of Christian Athletes and the National Honor Society. I was also the mascot for

my high school during my junior year. Between all these activities, my family, my friends,

homework and my animals, I do not have much time to spare. That is why time manage-

ment and prioritizing are so important to my life. At the top of my list of priorities is God.

The relationship that I have with God is the most important thing in my life. Without a

strong spiritual conviction, I would not be able to balance the many different activities that

I have chosen to become involved with.

My parents have taught me that to be successful, you must be well rounded. My dad

was a former 4-H member. He encouraged my sister and I to get involved with the 4-H pro-

gram as well as athletics and the FFA. I have been a member of 4-H since the third grade.

I know that no matter where I go in the state of Texas, that I will be able to find a 4-H or FFA buddy. I have made so many close friends through these organizations, it would be hard to imagine my life without them. My parents are the main reason that I have been able to juggle the activities in my life. Without their love and support, I am certain that I would have had great difficulty succeeding at any of my endeavors. Little did I know that I had not "learned it all" in preschool. Life has been an adventure and every phase is more exciting than the last one.

4-H Honors...

4-H Teen Council President...200-2001, 2002-2003

State 4-H Recordbook Winner...2002

Entomology Team, 2nd Place...2000

Gold Star...2001, Lubbock County

Fall, 2005

Dear Mr. Wallrath,

I was awarded a Houston Livestock Show and Rodeo Scholarship in the summer of 2003. It was truly an honor to be chosen as a 4-H Scholar. It has been so important that your generosity has made such a large contribution to so many young adults each year. I have always dreamed of attending Texas A & M University and thanks to your kind gift, that dream has become a reality. You, along with the 4-H Organization have helped so many to pursue a higher education.

Your contribution has been unbelievably beneficial to me as I attend Texas A & M University. I plan on majoring in Entomology. With a degree in Entomology, I hope to someday become a forensic entomologist. (Entomology is a branch of zoology that deals with insects) I am currently one month away from completing an internship working as a field technician for the Integrated Pest Management County Extension Agent in Lubbock County. He is a trained entomologist and I have learned a great deal under his tutelage.

My second semester at Texas A & M was better than the first. This semester, I joined collegiate 4-H. I hope to become very active in this organization in future semesters. This semester, it has become very obvious to me that my college experience will be something that I never will forget. Not only have I learned so much while I have been in college, I have been schooled on life in general. These experiences would not have been available to me without your contribution. I want you to know that! My grade point average is now a cumulative 3.0. It will get higher.

At the risk of repeating myself, I greatly appreciate your generous donation. It is almost beyond comprehension that there are strangers interested in making an investment in my education. Make no mistake about that. It is an investment because I plan to return the efforts to my own community once my education is completed. The world is a better place because of people like you. You changed my life and the lives of so many other scholarship recipients. Thank you, again!

Sincerely,

Emilie Hartfield

June 6, 2005

From The Texas 4-H Youth Development Foundation...

Dick Wallrath is one of the greatest supporters of 4-H in the nearly one hundred years of their history in Texas. In the past two years alone, Mr. Wallrath has donated two million dollars directly to fund our programs. This has been in addition to the livestock shows. Dick is a true believer in 4-H and the bright youth leaders it consistently produces. Dick has never hesitated to financially assist the 4-H youth of his state in attaining their goals and fulfilling their dreams. Dick Wallrath has given away more than 100 scholarships to high school seniors across the state. Dick is also a tremendous asset to the Texas 4-H Foundation Board of Trustees. The active role he has played in the decision making process of the Board has been a perfect example of the kind of leaders 4-H has hoped to produce for years to come. Dick is the "real deal." He has an amazing passion for kids...one that goes unmatched in the largest 4-H program in the United States. The Texas 4-H program is truly blessed to have Dick Wallrath at the helm of this organization as the need for strong leadership becomes more vital for the success and prosperity of this nation and for the continuation of the way of life we all cherish.

Jim E. Reeves

Executive Director

Texas 4-H Youth Development Foundation

CHAPTER 11

Chapter Eleven...The Ranch and Heaven's Gate

There is something much more than territorial about Texans and the special place they call home. The litany of Texas traditions and identifiable state characteristics is in a league of its' own. There is a purgatorial halo that hovers above every Texan. If you choose to question that adage, then just ask one. The Dallas Cowboys are America's Team. They have not won a Super Bowl in more than a decade, but ask anyone in Dallas. The Cowboys are to the NFL what the Longhorn wishbone offense was to college football. Texas is the state of icons and the state of symbols. Obviously, two of the last four presidents have come from Texas. From rebel country singers like Willie and Waylon to Frito pies and horny toads, the Lone Star State carries the badge of distinction above and beyond the call. From Grand Champion steers to the Stetson, from the legend of the Yellow Rose to the icy bite of an autumn storm called a blue norther, Texas is a state of mind. Explaining Texas pride is like explaining to a Yankee, what the number of x's means to a hat. It cannot be done. And nowhere does the notion of freedom and independence resonate louder than the ranch. Texas cattle barons flaunted their royalty on the mega-ranches of early Texas. Today, the ranch has remained a symbol of personal sovereignty. The oversized gate on the five-acre plot or the miles of crisscrossing barbed wire have been the badges of autonomy and why Henry David Thoreau explained the need to "live after your own nature." Dick Wallrath has lived with a list of goals since he put down the bottle almost four decades ago. The list has always been evolutionary, but one entry remained constant. Dick Wallrath would always reside on a ranch.

Centerville, Texas is located halfway between Dallas and Houston just off Interstate 45. The sign posted showed a population of 903. Thoughts of where more than 900 people lived in the sleepy, dry community have entered more than one mind as the town slipped by faster than a swarm of fire ants scurried up the nose of a grazing steer that disturbed their mound. Once past the Town Café and a courthouse that has seen much better days, the small modest ranch homes lined the rural route to Champion Ranch. Dick's ranch is not hard to locate. The manicured grass between the roadway and the fence line is the first signal that Champion Ranch was imminent. The pristine white fence hugged every inch of roadway acreage. The gates to the main entrance are not ostentatious. There are two modest stucco structures that are covered by Spanish tile roofs. The iron façade connecting the two structures carries the name of Champion Ranch. A small, mechanized gate prevents unwelcome visitors. The gate is open during the day on most weekdays. A small office complex is located directly inside the main gate. Dick's office is located inside the one story building. Dick's secretary, the ranch general manager and the cattle manager have offices inside the same building. Behind the office structure is a pasture that is home to six buffalo and a few scattered longhorn steers. The buffalo and the longhorns are nostalgic ranch candy. They look like western relics stolen from an era gone by. Dick bought the buffalo from an old friend who had died recently and asked Dick to take the animals and give them a peaceful home. The longhorns belong on a Texas ranch. They are not bound for the meat packer. The longhorns are Buckingham Palace guards, poised to greet the visitors to Champion Ranch.

Dick bought the property and mineral rights to what is now Champion Ranch in 1993. The purchase of what is now Champion Ranch was Dick's third ranch. Ranch ownership was a specific goal outlined after sobriety. The goals came from the book by Napoleon Hill called *Think and Grow Rich*. Champion Window Company had been the engine that drove the train. The true goals centered on ranch life and began many years before with the

Caney Creek beach house purchased down by the Gulf of Mexico. Dick wanted to be able to give his family a vacation retreat, however small it may have been. During the late sixties, Dick figured that a recovered alcoholic and a small business entrepreneur could build a small retreat near the water and help to rebuild some of the relationships that he missed during his drinking days. The "one dollar down, one dollar catch me" mortgage proved to be the first step in Dick Wallrath's goal driven property ownership.

The first ranch that Dick bought was located in the same general vicinity as Centerville. Dick's first ranch was 298 acres and was purchased in 1982 from Ray Addington. Two hours north of Houston, past the state prison at Huntsville, the rolling hills of Normangee and Madisonville provided the backdrop to Dick's first two forays into ranch ownership.

Dick Wallrath: My goals have always been associated with the ranches. Champion Window Company was the mechanism to drive me to the ranches. In 1982, business at Champion Window Company was growing faster than I ever imagined that it could. I needed the capital to re-invest in new equipment, a bigger staff and all the growth costs associated with expansion. In 1982, it was not the time to pull a big chunk out of the company and buy a ranch for my own personal satisfaction. My life was on a timetable. My goals were spelled out in black and white. The goal of owning a ranch with cattle was fast approaching. The delicate state of Champion Window Company would make the first goal out of reach. I told Ray Addington that I could not afford the ranch and that I would have to pass. Ray and I had known each other for years. He had me thrown in jail for passing a bad check when I was drinking. We became good friends after I got sober. He finally told me that him and his wife, Josie, wanted me to have that ranch. I explained again, that I could not pull that much money from the business. Maybe in a few years, I would be in a different position. Ray told me that I could buy the ranch for no money down and pay interest only for five years. It was two days before my goal to purchase a working ranch was about to expire. I had that property paid off well before the prescribed time line. I'll never forget the gesture and the opportunity provided by Mr. Addington.

The second ranch was purchased in 1988. The location was on Highway OSR near Madisonville, Texas. The ranch was fourteen hundred acres. The acquisition of Champion Ranch came in 1993. The land was owned by a family, primarily in the sugar beet business in Florida. The eldest son owned the property in Texas. Dick became aware of the property for sale and discovered more money had been borrowed against the property than the property was worth. The negotiations became frustrating to Dick Wallrath. He believed that solid, fair negotiations were impossible with someone that did not know the value of a dollar. Dick dug in his heels and pulled his offer from the table. The phone rang quickly. Champion Ranch was purchased for $750 per acre. The mineral rights were purchased for another half million dollars. The total land now covers almost six thousand acres. The ranch came with more than a dozen working oil wells. Production is still pumped into holding tanks adjacent to each pumping station. Oil company trucks come every two weeks to take the oil from the storage tanks. The ranch is issued a monthly check.

Dick has added many new structures to Champion Ranch since he purchased the property in 1993. The main house is new. The sprawling ranch is nestled against a seventy-five acre lake that Dick had built with the help of an army of engineers and architects. From a running creek on his property, Dick had constructed a 2200 foot damn that reached a height of fifty feet. The backed up water filled an expanse that was cleared by another army of earthmovers and LeTourneau type equipment. The result was a stunning manmade lake that served as the backdrop to the main house on the ranch. The main house was a personal project for both Patsy and Dick. Dick wallowed in the construction plans, the physical design, the choice of underlying materials and the support trusses necessary to create the wide open expanses inside the house. The ranch house was an eclectic mix of authentic Western architecture and stunning European granite. Inside the main living room was a skylight the size of some small states. The Texas star hovered high above the golden inner dome. The back family room was constructed entirely of glass. The lake swept around each of three sides to the massive entertainment room. Spectacular leather couches and a widescreen, drop down television gave a man the only room to rival the sports book at Caesar's Palace. Glass gun cases held the relics of a proud Texas past. Each bedroom was designed around one geographical territory of the West. One room was a Southwest design, highlighted by Aztec art and Native American paintings from Arizona and New Mexico. Another bedroom captured the beauty and fury of the Rocky Mountains. The master bedroom was a white Lone Star oasis that overlooked an infinity edged swimming pool. The grounds were meticulously cared for. Cactus blossoms filled each morning with a sunrise masterpiece. It was a painting in search of an artist. The guesthouse was built on the lake, as well. Almost thirty miles of paved roads traversed the ranch. Dick paved the roads to keep his trucks clean and because the ranch was much prettier without a cloud of road dust obstructing the view.

Just before Dick's mother passed away, Ruth Wallrath told her son that she had seen three white horses come to take her away. The horses and their riders were going to take her to heaven. She was at peace with those horses. On a long winding drive that was the only road to Dick's house, the cattle herds could be seen in the distance and the wind swept pasture leading up to the main house was calmly vacant. An occasional wolf or deer was often seen darting across the roadway. At the top of a long, gradual climb was a wooden gate and a solitary Texas flag. The main house was nowhere in sight. Just past the wooden gate and the Texas flag, the drive fell below the horizon and veered straight to the lake. Past the manicured lawn and cactus blossoms, the main house sat against the mirrored image of a glass covered painting. Off to the edge of the tree line and near the barbed wire separating the cattle from the main house stood three white stallions. The horses were never ridden and had free reign of the ranch grounds.

A close friend had heard the story of Ruth Wallrath and her three white horses. Warren Krisco rode a banana boat from Costa Rico to make his stake in the United States. Instead, he found the bottom of a bottle. Dick met Warren at the twelve-step program in Houston. They became good friends as they both discovered the rewards of sobriety. Warren worked in management at a local drug store chain and built an admirable estate worth well over a half million dollars. When Warren contracted cancer, he asked Dick Wallrath to act as the executor to his will. Reluctantly, Dick agreed to oversee the disbursement of Warren's estate. When Warren passed away, Dick discovered a specific amount of the money he was designated to disperse was destined for himself. Mr. Wallrath was directed to purchase three white horses. The horses were never to be ridden. The three white horses would be allowed to run free on the ranch forever. Dick had relayed to Warren, the story about his mother and her vision of three white horses coming to take her to heaven. Warren remembered the way Dick felt comfort in how his mother accepted death and embraced the here-after. Although they never spoke concerning Warren's link to Ruth Wallrath, Dick always knew that story had some value to Warren, especially during the latter stages of Warren's illness. The horses were a spiritual mechanism to secure the bond between mother and a son forever. The horses were to be turned out permanently. The wishes of a dying man were never ignored. The horses were purchased and given a lifetime pass to Champion Ranch. Today, three white horses roam the grounds at Champion Ranch. They graze casually along the miles of fence line inside the ranch. A Costa Rican expressed his gratitude and the omnipresence of maternal energy was sealed within a Texas bloodline.

The construction of new structures continued throughout the nineties on Champion Ranch. A new bunkhouse was built to house up to twenty. Next to the bunkhouse was a walk-in cooler for meat storage, a carving room for carcasses and a giant brick barbecue grill, stretching some six feet in length. Built next to the bunkhouse was a replica saloon, complete with kerosene lamps, an antique bar and seating for more than one hundred. Dick offered the grounds for a variety of events. Down the drive from the bunkhouse and saloon was a full-sized outdoor rodeo arena and a livestock sales arena building. The rodeo arena had bleachers for five hundred and room for a thousand more. The sales arena was a newly constructed air-conditioned display showcase for any bull sales, mare sales or livestock sales conducted on the premises.

Dick has built or is in the process of building homes for his ranch employees. Each full-time ranch employee has Dick's promise of a college education for their children and a fine home to raise them up in. Each home is a three-bedroom ranch with three bathrooms and a floor plan that covers nearly two thousand square feet. The home sites are carefully scouted to provide breathtaking views from every angle and to provide the private setting of a solitary estate. Dick is often seen on the rafters of the construction sites directing the home site construction himself. In the hot, humid Texas sun, Dick Wallrath isn't afraid to wield a hammer or a nail gun.

Champion Ranch has a General Manager and a Cattle Manager. Gary Robertson is the General Manager. Tuffy Loftin is the Cattle Manager. Gary was married to Dick's daughter Dina. (upcoming chapter) Gary's responsibilities include the entire ranch maintenance schedule and the physical appearance of the property. Gary has overseen countless new construction projects on the ranch and the endless progression of daily upkeep is staggering. Tuffy Loftin oversees the cattle operation, breeding, marketing, animal health and all livestock decisions. Dick hired Tuffy to run the cattle operation, not to hand hold him through the job. Dick and Tuffy met years ago, when Dick was purchasing cattle for his prior smaller ranches. Tuffy was raised in Southeast Texas, the son of an oil field worker and a hairdresser. Tuffy grew up a cowboy and learned the meaning of working a ranch at an early age. In 1983, Tuffy graduated from Texas A & M University with a degree in Agriculture Economics/Farming and Ranch management. Tuffy Loftin had been the cattle manager at three other ranches before Dick Wallrath offered him a job at Champion Ranch.

Tuffy Loftin: You rarely get a chance to work for one of your heroes. I had known Mr. Wallrath from my other ranch management positions. I had the opportunity to attend some social functions at Champion Ranch and jumped at the chance to work there when the offer materialized.

Champion Ranch is a cow/calf operation. The ranch maintains a specific inventory of cows and they are asked to manufacture one calf per year. Primarily, the offspring are sold. Champion will maintain a select few offspring as replacement heifers (female bovine less than two years old that have not borne a calf). At present, Champion Ranch has about two thousand head of cows, fifty bulls, twenty horses (ten mares and ten working geldings) and one stud horse. The two thousand head of cows should produce more than eighteen hundred calves each year, so at any one time there may be thirty-five to thirty-eight hundred animals on premise.

Calves are sold normally at seven months old. The bulk of the steers are placed for sale or market on video. Inferior heifers are sold like any other steer. For the non-Texans, a steer is a castrated bull. Inferior heifers are judged by experience. Cattle managers can tell by sight, that a certain cow will never amount to a breeding heifer. Those heifers are sold into the feeding industry like all other steers. They are fed up in weight and then slaughtered. Breeding bulls are good for seven or eight years. When they reach the age of shade, they begin to be interested in resting in the shade. They lose libido and it becomes hamburger time. That is how the food chain operates in the cattle business. The older cows are sold for slaughter. The older bulls are sold for slaughter. The weaker and smaller heifers are sold for slaughter at the same time as the young steers.

Commercial livestock is judged by the steer count. All commercial livestock is castrated at roughly three months old. The castration literally takes their mind off ass and puts it back on grass. Without testicles, the animal can concentrate on eating and not reproduction. The hormones of the animal are altered after castration. The meat will marble quicker. After the intake of food, the transformation into meat marble and muscle is different than that of a bull. The overall quality of meat comes from genetics. The most recognizable brand of beef is Angus. Champion Ranch raises Brangus cattle. The cross is between Brahman and Angus cattle. The Angus cattle are known for their texture and quality, but they normally could not stand up to the Texas heat. The Brahman cattle come from Southeast Texas and are known for their tolerance to the Texas heat. The combination produces quality meat that can stand up to the Texas summers. Older animals and certain breeds are ripe for processed meats like ground beef or hot dogs. Quality meats are HRI (Hotel Restaurant Industry) cuts.

There are four stages to the meat processing industry. Champion Ranch is one stop during the four stage process. Champion Ranch is the first stop, the cow/calf operation. Champion will raise and keep the cattle until the approximate age of seven months or six hundred pounds. The animals will leave the cow/calf operation for the stocker operation. There, the animals will be grazed and grass fed until they reach the nine hundred pound level. Next, they are sent to a feeder operation. The animals are confined and fed three times per day. They are corn-fed and this confined feeding continues until they reach the twelve hundred to fifteen hundred pound level. At that level, the cattle reach their killing weight. The meat packer is their last stop. Feeder operations are most likely to be near the slaughterhouses. Both operations are likely to be found within the corn producing states. The cost of shipping feed is prohibitive within the profit margins of the cattle industry.

Champion Ranch is expanding their own horse breeding operations. One stud can usually maintain a stable of twenty mares. Champion is pursuing the working ranch horse market. Many people seek a trained ranch horse that they can ride or use to perform certain ranch chores. They do not have the time or the expertise to break the horses themselves. A gelding sold for a working ranch horse will be schooled at Champion for a couple years before they are sold. Other markets include the roughstock horses for rodeos. Years ago, these were the horses that no one could ride. They were simply the bad horses. Today, the roughstock business is big business. A stud that bucks is worth big money inside the rodeo arena. After his career is over, the bucking stud is very valuable inside the stud market. A good bucking horse is worth up to ten times what a good ranch horse might command.

Overall, the operation at Champion Ranch is not one that Dick Wallrath undertook to do halfway. Then again, not many things in his life has he attacked halfway. Dick Wallrath never purchased Champion Ranch to be a spectator. From a morning ride on a ranch gelding to driving a tractor while clearing the rear perimeter of the ranch boundaries, Dick Wallrath took an active roll in every facet of ranch life. Dr. Phil Legget, age 51, could best describe the confrontation when the immovable force met the unbreakable spirit. Dr. Leggett has been a pioneer in Laproscopic surgery. Based in Houston, Texas, Dr. Leggett has been a personal friend to Dick Wallrath for years. They met in 1992, while Dr. Leggett was a member of the Steer Auction Committee at the Houston Livestock Show and Rodeo. Dr. Phil, as we like to call him, recalled an earlier incident that Dick had called about.

Dr. Leggett: The first real introduction to Dick Wallrath came when he relayed a story to me that I had some professional reservations about. Apparently, Dick had gone to visit a cardiologist about some shortness of breath and fatigue. The doctors ran extensive tests and came to the conclusion that Dick Wallrath needed bypass surgery. The arteries were blocked and the routine surgery could clear the obstruction. Dick balked at the notion of being cut open. He basically told the doctors to pound sand. That gosh darn hard headed

Wallrath went home, changed his eating habits, got more exercise and that was some ten years ago. His subsequent heart tests have showed clear sailing. I once fixed Wallrath's hernia through a Laproscopic procedure. While many patients lie around for days, Dick was working out the next day. The only other patient that I can recall like Dick was a Green Beret veteran who underwent a similar procedure. That man took part in a 24 mile bicycle ride on the day following his surgery. That display may have topped Dick Wallrath, but the man was thirty-five years younger.

Dr Leggett: Those stories are well and good, but the one that epitomizes Dick Wallrath happened four year ago. I got a call from Champion Ranch. Dick was calling me from the ground next to an oilrig on his property. I picked up my phone and answered.

"Hello."

"I just screwed up." Dick Wallrath announced through the phone.

"Where are you, Dick?" I asked.

"I am on the ground next to the tractor and I got a piss load of blood shootin out of my eye." Dick answered with no real panic in his voice.

"What happened?" I pushed on.

"I just screwed up, that's all. I was pissed off that the damn oil companies had not cut the grass around the rigs. I took the tractor up there and started cutting the grass myself. It is their responsibility. They had some barbed wire buried in the long grass and my tractor caught the wire and whipped it up over the tires. One end of the barbed wire struck me in the eye. I think it knocked my freeking eye out." Dick described the scene.

Dr. Leggett: I called for an ambulance immediately. The vehicle came out of Huntsville and traveled some forty miles north to Centerville. I called the ranch and told them to take the ambulance to the spot where Dick was located. As soon as we had Dick stable, I had him sent down to Houston where I could help get Dick the best medical treatment in the state. We did a CT on him and discovered that there was a chunk of wire lodged inside his eye that came within a fraction of an inch of killing him instantly. Dick lost his eye, but that was one tough sonofabitch!

Whether the ranch played host to a championship charity rodeo or a summer FFA Executive seminar, the immaculate grounds of the sleeping giant left an indelible impression on all. The ranch has been the sweet smell from a summer rain. Black cattle searched for the lazy shade of the rolling acres. The Texas sun climbed higher than the rippling waves of heat, lost in a hazy, yellow galaxy. The ranch can change faster than a summer lightning surge. Texas is the stage for nature's most violent creations and the storms roll in like an avalanche of Guadalupe Peak boulders. Black clouds roll in like thundering cavalry divisions. Lazy summer afternoons become churning battlefields of colliding low-pressure fronts. Central Texas weather is a version of Texas Hold 'Em. You never know what you're going to get until you sit through it. The beauty of nature is not only the neon-like red glow of a late summer sunset, but the call to arms in a sudden squall, the explosion of power and the helpless nature of the witness. Nowhere in the world is the view more exquisite than the ranch.

Thunderstorms ignite the flatlands with horizontal lightning. Water torrents fall like sheets of glass shattered in heaven. Tornadoes churn up the dry clay like sand and reduce farm equipment to windswept clutter. Hardened cowboys stand in awe. Nature has no complacency level.

Summer droughts stretch on endlessly. The ranch is tested each day and each year. In Texas, the ranch remains. Dick Wallrath remains at the ranch.

CHAPTER 12

Chapter Twelve...The Texas FFA and Dick Wallrath

Background FFA facts:

National FFA Organization...founded 1928

The Texas FFA Foundation...founded 1929.

2004-2005 National FFA Organization Membership...476,732

2004-2005 Texas FFA Foundation Membership...61,000 (2nd largest state FFA organization next to California at 63,700)

Founded in 1928, the Future Farmers of America brought together students, teachers and the stalwarts of agricultural business education. The National FFA Organization is committed to the individual student growth by providing educational opportunities through the growing number of scholarships awarded and the dedicated mantra of the members, staffers and executives to continually infuse agriculture into the classroom. The National FFA Organization is a shining example of what is right with education. Members are prepared for leadership and success through participation, job training, classroom education and diverse interaction with their peers. The primary goal of FFA is student success.*

FFA is not an elective. The program combines classroom instruction and hands-on opportunities called supervised agricultural experiences (SAEs). These programs include activities such as starting a business or working for an established company.*

FFA holds a federal charter. Last year, FFA awarded $1.9 million in scholarships. One out of every eight applicants received a scholarship.*

FFA members can be found in every community in America. From metropolitan Chicago and New York City to the smallest community in Texas or Oklahoma, students in grades 7-12 are eligible for FFA. More than 70% of all members come from rural non-farm, urban and suburban areas. FFA programs are funded by private donations and corporate sponsorships at the local, state and national levels.*

*...www.ffa.org

Dick Wallrath and the Texas FFA

By Aaron Alejandro, Executive Director of the Texas FFA Foundation

June 16, 2005

Building the relationship with Dick Wallrath and the Texas FFA Foundation has been one of the most exciting experiences of my professional life. Although trite, trying to capture in words the experiences that have led us to our current relationship will surely fall short in painting the picture of the little things, which make him and his philanthropic relationships unique. Allow me to simply state, you will always know where you stand with Dick Wallrath. In addition, I believe that Dick is one of the finest examples of the old adage, you don't have to be loud to be heard. Allow me to briefly describe how we met, his generosity and the philosophies we share. These shared beliefs have helped to serve as the glue for a great working relationship.

Terry Phillips, Director of Agricultural Education in the Texas Education Agency (TEA), called me one day to make me aware of a gentleman who was looking to make an investment in the Texas 4-H program and may be considering a similar gift to the Texas FFA Foundation. I quickly called and set a meeting with the "King of the Steer Buyers", according to Philanthropy World Magazine. I drove to Centerville, Texas the evening before our scheduled meeting. I wanted to be rested and prepared for our first meeting.

I arrived at Champion Ranch about fifteen minutes before our meeting. In proper attire, I did not have to wait long. Within minutes, a secretary announced that Mr. Wallrath would see me. As I entered his office, I was struck by the Texas history and cowboy memorabilia covering every inch of his office. Sitting back in a leather executive chair was the "King of the Steer Buyers" himself. Mr. Wallrath was wearing a cowboy hat, a black tank top, jeans and boots. The man was in splendid physical condition. He met me with a firm handshake and a warm smile. The handshake didn't try to define the person. So many men feel the need to define by their machismo by the pressure of a handclasp. We enjoyed coffee and began to visit about life, our organizational philosophies, our personal philosophies and what makes our state and country great.

After our initial visit, Mr. Wallrath gave me a tour of Champion Ranch and his Brangus operation. Driving around the ranch gave a great opportunity to look into the soul of Dick Wallrath. As he drove around the ranch and described his prized possession, you could quickly see the passion he had as an individual to be a steward of all that is placed in his care. Mr. Wallrath recounted several stories as we toured the ranch, where in business and with his personal resources, that he has never been able to out give God. Remember, I said that you do not have to be loud to be heard. That drive around the ranch spoke volumes as to the man I would be working with and the relationship to come for Texas FFA and young people around the state.

We concluded our first meeting and set up another meeting in three weeks. At that meeting, we were to work out the details of a gift to the Texas FFA Foundation from Mr. Wallrath. I was eager to meet again, but not simply to arrange the financial investment, but because I was also inspired by Mr. Wallrath's passion for life, and his desire to make things better for so many young people. We scheduled our meeting and I was anxious to get back to Champion Ranch.

On the way back to Champion Ranch some weeks later, I met a colleague of mine for lunch in Dallas. In my vehicle, I had all of the collateral material to share with Mr. Wallrath. The information helped to define why a gift to the Texas FFA Foundation would be greatly appreciated and what steps the foundation would take to ensure the gift would be used as Mr. Wallrath intended. While at lunch in Dallas, my car was broken into and everything was stolen. My wallet, my computer, my brief case and a host of other items were all stolen. In addition, the glass throughout the car was shattered. In the heat of the Texas summer, I was going to make that meeting in Centerville. When I arrived at Champion Ranch, Mr. Wallrath was very kind. He had some ranch employees cover my windows with plastic and invited me to stay at the guesthouse on the ranch. I was leaving for Houston the next morning, so the invitation was a welcome end to a difficult day. We drove to Buffalo, Texas to pick up some pizza. We visited about the Texas FFA Foundation that evening and he felt very comfortable that an investment in our program was an investment in our young people. He would call me a few weeks later to come down and pick up the check.

Getting to know Dick Wallrath has been rewarding in that we share many similar philosophies. I grew up at Cal Farley's Boys Ranch. That experience has given me a special appreciation for ranch life and the value of hard work. Dick Wallrath became a successful businessman because he had the tenacity and drive to make it happen. He wasn't without struggles, both personally and professionally, but who is? Dick Wallrath exuded resiliency, a character trait that Texas FFA proudly promotes. Once, when we were visiting, I recalled the story of a downtrodden man who said, "I wish I could find a place where I no longer had storms in my life." I told the man that I could take him there. I could take him to a place where it never rains and nothing grows. I could take him to the desert. Show me someone with some rain in their lives and some resiliency to navigate through the rain and I will show you a person who is destined to grow. Dick Wallrath has grown through the many storms of his life and has now become a steward to all that was entrusted to him. The bible says, to whom much is given, much is expected. Dick Wallrath is ensuring others will have the opportunity because of his success and passion to give back to society.

I relayed to Mr. Wallrath my story of why I value and appreciate the Texas FFA. I shared my personal story of loss, struggle, resiliency and success. The Texas FFA gave me the opportunity to be the first person from my family to receive a college degree. During my career, I have had the opportunity to work with a nonprofit organization, which dealt with at-risk young people and families. My job required that I work at a maximum-security prison, in a boot camp-like environment for young people and I was able to work with truant offenders.

Once in a rural town, I was listening to a discussion by some older gentlemen about what was wrong with this country. They said that what was wrong with our country was that we had to get back to basics. We had to get back to the three R's, reading, writing and arithmetic (also know as the three R's). As I listened, I finally decided to engage the conversation. I told them of my work with truant offenders, boot camps and inmates at various prisons. I explained that all of the young people I dealt with could read, write or do math at some functional level. Unfortunately, the struggles they faced in life, which served to facilitate their predicament were not related to basic educational skills but related to something much greater, values. I insisted that the three R's missing were not reading, writing and arithmetic but respect, responsibility and resolution. The problems facing our nation had to do with teaching our young people to respect themselves and their fellow man, be responsible for their own actions and learn to resolve conflict rather than battle it. Families and communities would reap the benefits from those values. Success, happiness and meaningful employment are all a direct result of the values laid as the foundations within childhood.

While sharing the story with Mr. Wallrath, I saw a smile come to his face. Mr. Wallrath believes strongly in the principals of the three R's, respect, responsibility and resolution. Scholarships will mean nothing if the student does not offer respect for the source of his opportunity by taking the responsibility and resolution to work hard and turn the gift of an education into the backbone of a career. Mr. Wallrath and I also shared a another common philosophy as it related to agriculture.

I once asked, "What separates the Texas FFA from other youth organizations? Do we think that we are the only organization where leadership and positive life skills are schooled into every member?" Tough questions. After some serious thought, I was taken back to my dorm parent at Boys Ranch. Mr. Winston Chandler taught me many things about life, jobs and agriculture. My son's name is Chandler, so the influence that this man had on my life was more important to me than I could ever explain on paper. Mr. Chandler would not allow any boys in his dorm to work at any job other than an ag related job. At Boys Ranch, there were many jobs unrelated to agriculture. There were jobs at the dining room or at different school facilities. Many of those jobs were warm in the winter and cool in the summer. Mr. Chandler would have none of that. I remember vividly when a strong winter blizzard came to the plains of Texas while I was a student at Boys Ranch. I was given a sledgehammer by Mr. Chandler and told to drive to the other side of the ranch where a water tank for the horses was located. I was told to bust up the ice from that tank to free up the water for those horses. I protested to deaf ears. It was colder than I could ever remember in Texas. Mr. Chandler asked me if I got thirsty when it got cold outside. I responded that I did. "Well then, darlin, don't you think that those horses might get thirsty too?" What a life lesson, as simple as it sounded. Mr. Chandler explained that if we do not do our jobs, something dies. We simply do not let a teammate down or a fellow employee down, we kill something. Our failure in an ag job kills an animal, a crop, a person, a community, a state or a county.

The Teaxs FFA has appreciated and honored Mr. Wallrath's gifts in many ways. First, we endowed the Texas FFA Star Awards through a memorial to his late daughter, Dina. Annually, the Dina Wallrath Robertson Memorial Star Awards are given to sixteen young people who have excelled in their agricultural science projects and enterprises. We have endowed twenty AgriScience Fair scholarships and sixteen proficiency award scholarships as a direct result of Mr. Wallrath's philanthropy.

In total, Mr. Wallrath has invested more than $1.5 million in the young people of the Texas FFA to date. This level of giving makes Mr. Wallrath the largest all-time donor in the seventy-seven year history of the Texas FFA. We hope the message has been received that we honor and appreciate everything he has done for our organization. We honor not only the magnitude of the generosity, but the humble manner by which he carries himself.

You do not have to be loud to be heard! Mr. Wallrath will be heard. His name will echo in perpetuity and eternity thanks to his generosity. Many communities, our state and the nation will be a better place to live, work and raise our families as a result of Mr. Wallrath's support and investment in the young people of Texas.

With much respect to a friend, mentor and philanthropist, respectfully submitted:

Aaron Alejandro

Executive Director

Texas FFA Foundation

Austin, Texas

Aaron Alejandro...

Two children, son, Chandler and daughter, Abigail

Executive Director, Texas FFA Foundation

Graduate of Cal Farley's Boys Ranch, Amarillo, Texas

Past President of the Texas FFA Foundation (Texas' largest youth organization and the only

Hispanic to be elected to that position)

Texas Department of Agriculture, consultant

CEV Multimedia, Ltd., marketing and sales, produced Life Strategies, Leadership Series,

Power of Choice and Fundamental Parliamentary Procedure videotapes.

District Director for a member of the United States Congress.

Texas Tech University, graduate/Agricultural Education

Board of Directors, Boys and Girls Club and Rotary Club, Witchita Falls, Texas

1990 Texas Spokesperson for Agriculture

Apprentice Instructor Level III, Warriors Way Martial Arts Academy, Jun Fan Gung Fu,

Muay Thai kick boxing, Kali/Silat, Sayoc Kali, and Giron Escrima.

Director of Executive Self-Defense (ESD), private appointment only

CHAPTER 13

Chapter Thirteen...Finding Dina and Finding Dad

Dina Denise Wallrath Robertson lost her valiant battle with Non-Hodgkin's Lymphoma on September 5, 1993. Dina was thirty-one years old. She was survived by her husband, Gary, her son, Alexander, her father and mother, Dick and Betty, two brothers, Danny and Michael, and two sisters, Joni and Pam. The youngest of five children, Dina was affectionately called Deede by her parents, brothers and sisters.

Dick Wallrath: I have never believed in a vindictive God. I cannot believe that God sits in judgement of our lives and thus dispenses the appropriate sadness and heartache to those judged to be unappreciative of the gifts he has provided. God took my daughter because he didn't want her to suffer anymore. He wanted her to be in a better place and I thank him for that. Deede got sick and those things are not part of God's master plan. They just happen. Of course, there were more than a few nights when I cussed at God for taking my Deede. I wanted to know why he didn't take a mean old, crusty man like me instead. She had her whole life ahead of her and Deede was sweeter than a candy cane resting in a bowl of honey. I know now that God is not responsible for every child that dies in this world. Things happen good and bad that do not fall under the heading of God's will. I'd like to wring the neck of every preacher that starts every child's eulogy with it was God's will.

Dina Denise Wallrath was born on October 14, 1961, the youngest of the Wallrath children. When Deede was born, Pam was six, Joni was eight, Danny was ten and Michael was twelve. Deede excelled in school and showed a domestic side at a very young age. Dick was still drinking when his youngest daughter was born. Deede had three mothers and

179

three fathers while growing up. The separation of ages between Deede and the older siblings worked as a protective blanket wherever Deede went. From the Galena Park Junior High School mascot to her days in College Station, Deede had her brothers and sisters to watch over her.

Pam Wallrath Dolenz: I remember quite vividly when Deede was born. I was not happy about it. I was perfectly content to remain the baby of the house. I was not thrilled with relinquishing that title. Deede was ten years old when dad quit drinking. She was always the moderator between mom and dad. I saw dad and Deede grow close after he quit drinking and that bond had an effect on how Deede viewed the divorce. Most of us were out of the house and married when dad quit drinking. I think we all had some pretty rough memories of dad's drinking days, but Deede was the only one of us to have the balance of sobriety in her relationship with dad.

Dick Wallrath: When Deede was in high school, her class began to study alcoholism. Deede asked me to come to her school and give a speech to the kids. I was thrilled that she asked. Afterwards, I felt bad. I felt like I had embarrassed my daughter. Deede would have none of that. She was thrilled to have me come to the high school and she was very proud that I was willing to do it.

Through the years, Deede exhibited a very domestic side. She could sing like an angel, but excelled more at today what would be considered domestic tasks. Deede loved to sew, cook and work around the garden and yard. She never apologized for what she enjoyed and

180

that was the confidence that simply came from the heart. Deede did not live her life to impress others. She was thrilled to become pregnant and gave up her sales career in a heart-beat. There would be no day care centers in her life.

Deede loved being pregnant. She never felt self-conscious about gaining weight. She exercised every day and was totally consumed by eating properly. Deede was never a junk food fan and out of all the Wallrath children, she was by far the most health conscious. Irony was not an explanation for Deede's illness. The bible and every frame of spiritual wisdom contradicted the sequence of events surrounding Deede's life and the tragic illness that ended her life. After all, who could explain night after night, why a ten-year old girl would wait up until after midnight on a school night to cook her well-oiled father a good meal?

Dick Wallrath: Kids today have one major problem. They don't know where in the hell they are going. If you don't know where you are going then how in the hell are you going to get there? Kids go through college and think they will get hit on the head with a bolt of lighting. That bolt of lighting will be their calling card to wealth, fame and fortune. Well, it doesn't work like that. Young people need a good plan and unselfish goals to achieve where it is in life that they wish to travel. Deede always had unselfish goals. Deede enjoyed assisting her mother and father in whatever was asked of her. She never worked at being a good friend and sister to her siblings. That came naturally. Deede committed to a man she loved. She and Gary were married. Next, she devoted herself to the gift from God in her life, her son, Alexander Thomas. You see, God wants to be proud of us. When you pick a worthwhile goal, then God will help you achieve it. When you pick a selfish, narcissistic, search for whatever suits your path, then you, my friend, are on your own. Every so often, God has to insert someone into our lives that can be a beacon of what his vision has always been. God has to give us someone who does not need a halo hovering above, to know which direction to turn. Every so many years, someone is born without a selfish bone. God gave us Deede.

Deede attended Klein High School, north of Houston. After high school, Deede continued with her education at Texas A & M University. Her major was accounting and like everything else, Deede attempted, her grades in college reflected her attention to the task at hand. After three years of college, Deede approached her father and told him that college was not for her anymore. Accounting was not the direction she wished her life to take. Deede announced to her father that she wanted to go to work for the window company and become a window salesperson.

Prior to leaving school, Dina (as Gary always called her) met Gary Robertson at a College Station watering hole. Gary was raised in Tomball, Texas just north of Houston. Gary was active in FFA and high school football. After high school, Gary attended and graduated from Southwest Texas State University in San Marcos, Texas. Gary graduated in 1978. After graduation, Gary went to work for an oil company selling rock bits. Part of his sales territory included College Station, Texas. Dina and Gary met one night while Dina was on a date with someone else.

Gary Robertson: I bird-dogged that girl all night and finally got her phone number. The next day, I sent roses and we started seeing each other. I never did meet the guy she was with that first night. I can't imagine that he was real pleased with me. Dina was gorgeous and I had to meet her. The fact that she was with another guy apparently never deterred me that night. We started seeing each other in 1982. I spent a year in Africa for my company and a year in Singapore. I truly wanted to bring Dina with me, but those locales were not the place for a beautiful young lady. Dina and I kept our relationship strong through those two years overseas. We were married in Houston in 1985.

Dick Wallrath: What the hell was I wasting all that money on at Texas A & M if my daughter didn't want to be in school? I looked at her when she informed me that she wanted to go to work for Champion Window Company, and I thought that this girl was crazy. A sobering (I use that term sparingly) thought, was my daughter being subjected to the many Texas construction sites that window salesmen had to visit. The vivid picture of my baby daughter surrounded by those cigar-smoking, testosterone juiced, skirt-happy predators masquerading as builders made my skin crawl. I had flash thoughts of storming the construction sites wielding a twelve-gauge shotgun in search of the low down, piece of crap that insulted my daughter. I had flash thoughts of that happening all over Houston and San Antonio. The reality was, Deede handled that job like everything else in her life. She handled it with dignity, tenacity and class. Deede became one the top producing sales people at Champion within a short period of time. When it came time to be a mother, Deede informed me that her time as a sales person was complete and she had other responsibilities to attend to. Deede quit working to become a full-time mother.

Pam Wallrath Dolenz: Deede and I never wanted to place our children in day care centers. There are terrific day care centers all over the country, but our choice was not to place the babies in day care. We were fortunate to be able to work as full-time mothers. Daddy helped Deede with some financial obligations when she first quit working. Gary was working hard and the loss of the income from the window company had to be covered initially. Pregnancy agreed with Deede. She never worried about weight gain. She exercised every day while she was pregnant. When Alexander was born, I swear, Deede made us all think about our own paternal inadequacies. Deede made her own baby food. Honest! Deede used to take those old ice cube trays and fill them with diced vegetables and meat. Before each meal, she would defrost a certain food group and place the contents in a food processor. The groups contained celery, broccoli, carrots, chicken, etc. I rolled my eyes every time I watched her prepare those meals, but that was Deede. Some women throw organic cooking and natural lifestyle around like Prada and Gucci. Deede could not have cared less if anyone was impressed, annoyed or analytical about the choices she made concerning Alexander. Deede was just sweet. When I look into the eyes of Alexander, I see my sister. Alexander inherited those sweet eyes.

Gary Robertson: When I met Dick Wallrath, we jawed pretty good from the get-go. He let me know, in no uncertain terms, that he expected his baby girl to be treated well. I assured him that would be the case from day one. It was not in your best interest to be less than truthful with Dick Wallrath. I adored Dina and treating her well was not a chore but a privilege.

Alexander Thomas was born on November 25, 1990. Thomas was Gary's father's name and his own middle name. Alexander was a name to convey strength. The first name came down to a choice between Alexander and Maximillian. Alexander or A.T. won out and spared the young man a lifetime of schoolyard brawls. Gary and Alexander reside on the grounds at Champion Ranch, today. Gary is the Ranch Manager. Gary re-married two years after Dina passed away. Bonnie and Gary have raised a kind, strong young man.

Gary Robertson: After my wife died, my biggest concern was how to be the best parent to Alexander and how to do it so his mother would be proud. Traveling was out of the question. When Dick approached me about the position at the ranch, I knew that would be the best place for Alexander. I was blessed to meet Bonnie and never planned on finding any-one so special after I lost someone so special. I guess things have a way of working out. I'm sure Dina had a hand in where we all landed.

Dina Wallrath first began to experience intestinal problems sometime during 1991. The many doctors were baffled for many months. Pam remembered the first time she was aware of Deede's health problems came from a fainting episode at Deede's home. Deede passed out one day inexplicably. Alexander was very young and wound up on top of his mother as she lay motionless at home. A neighbor was summoned and Deede was taken to the hospital. Further tests resulted in the removal of Deede's gall bladder. After the gall bladder surgery, Deede's condition seemed to stabilize. The undiagnosed symptoms returned quickly. Fatigue, weight loss, night sweats and organ dysfunction were gradual clues to a larger problem.

Pam Wallrath Dolenz: I can recall when we were all due to go to see Gary, Deede and Alexander. Deede was going to have the entire family to her house for a summer get-together. I was on the phone with Deede when I could hear her struggle with each breath. Deede had to stop after each sentence and catch her breath. I told her to call a doctor immediately and get that checked out. She called Gary and they went to see the family doctor.

Gary Robertson: We all went to Sea World in San Antonio or some water park. Dina had trouble lifting A.T. and A.T. was not even eighteen months old. The shortness of breath and unusual fatigue continued to add to our concern. Once we met with our doctor following these recurring symptoms, a full chest x-ray revealed our worst fears. Cancer had invaded Dina's chest. The mass was pressing hard against her lungs, which was causing the shortness of breath. The cancer had taken over the lymph nodes throughout her upper body. After countless sessions with the oncologists, we were head up against one of the worst forms of malignant cancer.

Lymphomas are cancers of the lymphatic system, the body's blood filtering tissues that help to fight infection and disease. Like other cancers, lymphomas occur when cells divide too much and too fast. Growth control is lost and the lymphatic cells may overcrowd, invade and destroy lymphoid tissues and spread to other organs. There are two general types of lymphomas, Hodgkin's and non-Hodgkin's lymphoma. Hodgkin's disease contains specific cells, Reed-Sternberg cells, that are not found in any other cancerous lymphoma. Unlike Hodgkin's disease, non-Hodgkin's is comprised of ten different subtypes and twenty different disease entities. These subtypes are grouped into three biologic states, low grade, intermediate grade and high grade lymphomas. Non-Hodgkin's lymphoma is a heterogenous disease or a disease made up of non-similar parts. There will be as many as 50,000 new cases of NHL (non-Hodgkin's lymphoma) this year with as many as 25,000 deaths.* The difference between Hodgkins and Non-Hodgkins cancer is significant. In

Hodgkins, the cancer cells are relegated to one form of cancer cells. The chemotherapy and radiation treatment can be directed to kill the one form of cancer detected. With Non-Hodgkins cancer, the cells are from multiple forms of cancer and the success rate to reduce those cancer cells is significantly lower. Deede had non-Hodgkin's lymphoma. The general consensus of the cancers specialists in San Antonio and the countless others consulted from across the country, was that Dina Wallrath Robertson was in for the fight of her life.

After the initial shock of the diagnosis, the reality was that the cancer had advanced very quickly and the options were quickly fading. Chemotherapy and radiation had some limited initial success against the cancer. Following the chemotherapy and radiation treatments, there had been some hope that Dina was on her way to recovery. She was allowed to go home at that point. Dina and Gary were able to attend a company function for Gary, held in Dallas. It was 1992 and Dina had displayed remarkable courage and resolve to fight the disease and to beat it. Gary and Dina attended the company function in Dallas. Dina wore a wig because she had lost her hair during the radiation and chemotherapy. Dina looked radiant as she and Gary enjoyed a rare evening free from the treatment center in San Antonio. When they got back to the hotel, Dina announced that she had discovered a lump on her breast. After they returned home, the prognosis was again devastating. The cancer had returned and the only option left was a bone marrow transplant.

The treatments served to knock Dina's immune capabilities down to nothing. Dina fought like a valiant soldier. Often, she would rationalize that because the family had been very healthy for years, the odds were against her to follow the same path. Pamela and Joni took turns at the hospital. Gary never wavered in his prayers and faith that Dina would eventually recover. Despite the medical predictions, the Wallrath clan and Gary never gave up hope that Dina would recover. The toll on Dina was great. She was not a large person, physically. The drugs and the recurring nature of the cancer dug in to take every sliver of spirit from the small body they had been attacking. The immediate family and the medical family bonded as one. Together, they discovered what the true meaning of an overused, but poignant cliché really meant.

It is not the size of the dog in the fight, but the size of the fight in the dog!

Journalists and broadcasters throw around the terms associated with battle like they were casual adjectives attained daily and without much more sacrifice than battling through nine innings on a hot day or fighting fatigue on a basketball court for a multi-million dollar pay day. Terms associated with battle should be reserved for those battling for their lives. The brave men and women who are risking their lives to defend the way of life we cherish are warriors and heroes. The men, women and children who have been battling fatal diseases within their own bodies are warriors and heroes. Too many times, these soldiers are forgotten and their battles are trivialized or ignored. No one displayed more dignity and spirit in her battle with cancer than Dina Wallrath Robertson. Military analogies were not misplaced when they were used to describe the courage and unflappable poise associated with the blue-eyed Texas bulldog, determined not to lie down for any pragmatic pessimist or percentage based medical opinion. Dick Wallrath and Gary Robertson learned a great deal about strength and courage during those difficult days.

Dick Wallrath: I could see that the chemotherapy and radiation were not working the way we all had prayed for. When Deede lost her hair, she was mildly concerned about her future public forays. I gave her three hundred dollars and told her to buy a great wig and she

188

would look fabulous. Someone stole that money from her hospital room. I told her not to worry about the money, but Deede was so upset that someone would steal from someone else in the hospital. She didn't care about the wig, she still believed in the goodness of those around her. God, I learned more from my daughter in her thirty-one years than from a lifetime of born-again losers that don't look to God for assistance, but look to God for blame. They write off their misfortune or wasted years as God's plan. Deede looked to God for companionship, not crutches.

Dick Wallrath: When Deede was going through her radiation and chemotherapy, I sat with her and together, we fixed all that was ill with society. As my years have advanced so has my hairline. Rising hairline or not, I retained my long hair. My daughter hated the pony-tail that I wore and never failed to remind me of that fact on each and every visit to the hospital. Well, I eventually made a deal with Deede from that hospital room. On the day that she walked out of the hospital, Deede could take a scissors and cut that sonofabitch ponytail off my head. That day never came. When Deede died, I cut that sonofabitch pony-tail off. At Deede's funeral, I placed an envelope in her little hand. Inside that envelope was that ponytail.

The final hope was a bone marrow transplant. Bone marrow transplantation involves mov-ing the healthy stem cells from a donor's bone marrow into the veins of the patient. The new stem cells can travel through the bloodstream to the patient's bone cavities. Stem cells are cells that can produce red blood cells, white blood cells and platelets. Bone marrow transplantation allows the patient to receive high doses of chemotherapy or radiation because it replaces those cells destroyed by the various treatments. If the transplantation is successful, the newly injected cells should be free of cancer and capable of producing healthy cells.

Removal of the bone marrow from the donor is called harvesting. It takes place inside an operating room. A hollow syringe is used to remove one to two quarts from the donor's hipbone. The donor marrow is filtered through a small flexible catheter into a large vein inside the patient's chest. It may take a month for the bone marrow to begin functioning properly. Outside of bone marrow transplantation, surgery is rarely a treatment for NHL.**

Pamela was a close match for Deede, but Joni was a perfect match. Not long after the bone marrow transplantation, the signs were positive that the new blood cells and platelets were being produced. The toll, however, had been too great on such a small frame. The tremendous doses of chemotherapy and radiation had left Deede weak. At the young age of thirty-one, Dina Wallrath Robertson passed away on September 5,1993.

Gary Robertson: Dina left something that I can see every day. She left her compassion and her spirit in our son. I see that every time I look at Alexander. There is not a mean bone in that boy's body. I know that comes from his mother and I know that she would be so proud of him today.

Alexander Thomas Robertson: I will always remember my mother. We had very little time together, but I will cherish that time as a gift. There is so much I would like to ask her and so much I could tell her. I will someday.

Dick Wallrath: I never believed for a minute that Deede wouldn't pull through the disease.

During those last few days, I used to rub her feet and I know that she smiled at me through her eyes. I heard all the predictions and percentages, but I knew that Deede would pull through. When she didn't pull through, me and God were going to have a problem. In all the prayers and favors I have asked from God, he has never spoken to me or come to me in a vision. What he has done is guide me in the right direction. After Deede died, I couldn't sleep through a single night. I was not eating right. My health was sliding downhill faster than a greased fireman on a chrome plated fire pole. I was driving back to the ranch one night and I heard a Dolly Parton song on the radio. The song was *I Will Always Love You*. I had to pull over to the side of the road. I was crying like a baby. I couldn't get a handle on my daughter's death. I couldn't understand why her life was cut short and why my life hung on. I would have made that trade in a heartbeat.

Dick Wallrath: Remember Warren Krisco. My friend with cancer, who had me purchase the three white horses to turn out at the ranch. Warren asked me to go to Costa Rica with him because he had heard of a church up in the mountains that gave cancer patients a new opportunity to fight their disease. I agreed to go with Warren to Costa Rica. When we finally reached the church he searched for, there were many people waiting for a chance to speak at the alter, While we waited for Warren's turn, Deede appeared before me clear as a morning sunrise in Texas. Deede was wearing a white dress and it was billowing in the wind. She looked gorgeous. Deede was giggling and her golden hair was long and waving with the wind. Deede told me that everything was fine. She was happy. All I had to do was to take care of the family.

I slept that night for the first time in months. I realized that God was not through with me yet. He had some other issues for me to address. God knew that my daughter would have suf-fered greatly if she was allowed to stay where she was. God helped stop the suffering. I am not psychic and I will be happy to step outside with anyone who can find a way to denigrate what I saw. I know what I saw and what I saw was my daughter. God didn't want my Deede to suffer anymore, so he came and got her. She finally came back to me and don't ever tell me that those bright blue eyes and that smile were not my daughter.

Pam Wallrath Dolenz: Deede didn't stop with her visit to dad. She came to my house not long after she spoke to daddy. I remember one night when my ex-husband Buzz, heard me crying. When he got back to bed, there were two angels floating in our room. They had white dresses and golden hair. My son Garrett came to my room the next morning and told me that there was a lady in his room last night. She was in the corner and she had a white dress on. She left under the door. Buzz and I never told Garrett a single word about what Buzz told me he had witnessed in our bedroom. Garrett was eleven years old. Deede came to visit. You cannot tell me that angels only exist as a figment of my imagination.

The ability to conceive children is often confused with being a parent. No other indeli-ble mark on the planet is more important than our children and the compassion we instill in their hearts. It can be the mark of a great society when the middle masses respect the outer reaches of each generation. The older members of society are cherished for their wis-dom and hard work. The younger children of society are cherished for their promise and innocence. In a perfect world, God created man within the mirror of his own reflection. There is no more impossible concept to imagine than the rationalization of our own flaws as a pious excuse to place the blame for our own failures on some ephemeral deity. God certainly gave man the ability to accept the goodness within us all. The souls of angels pass down through us all. There is no explanation or caustic pattern to justify where, why or when the decision is made to leave an angel on the ground when another has been called back. Texas knew her as Dina Denise. Her family knew her as Deede. Texas has her again. His name is Alexander.

Dick has chosen many avenues to remember his youngest daughter. Among them are the scholarships awarded by the Texas FFA Foudation. One group of award scholarships based on involvement is the Star Awards. Members receiving Star Awards excel in their chosen fields and are the cream of the crop. Dick Wallrath felt these qualities embodied all of the characteristics of his daughter, the late Dina Wallrath Robertson. Dina was loveable and excelled in everything she did from academics to cheerleading. She was a dedicated daughter, sister, wife and mother. Dick Wallrath chose to endow sixteen Star Awards in Dina's memory.

*...www.oncologychannel.co   **...healthinfo.healthgate.com

CHAPTER 14

Chapter Fourteen...Scholarship #6 Kristin D. Dew

Dear Mr. Wallrath,

My name is Kristin Dew and I can proudly say that I am a "2000 4-H Scholar!" I was awarded a Houston Livestock Show and Rodeo Scholarship on June 13, 2000 and I am writing to express my great appreciation for your generosity toward the education of the youth in Texas. I was ecstatic when it was announced that I would be receiving $10,000. The award will help me out greatly because I will be able to focus more attention on my schoolwork and less time working at a job to pay for college.

I have chosen to attend Angelina College in Lufkin, Texas, which is a small community college close to my home. I made my decision to attend Angelina College because of their top rated nursing program. I plan to get into the nursing program and finish at AC with my Associate's Degree. I then plan to transfer to Stephen F. Austin State University where I will continue my nursing studies to earn my Bachelor's Degree and begin work as a registered nurse. I always wanted to do something in the medical field, but I was certain about my decision to be a nurse only a few months ago after losing my grandfather to heart disease. I watched how the nurses took care of him and gave him all the love and nurturing support they could. They really touched my heart. I saw the sparkle in my grandfather's eye when one nurse in particular came in to care for him. She would always try to make him smile and no matter how bad he was feeling, she was always successful. This nurse was my grandfather's ray of hope and someday, I would like to be that ray of hope to my patients.

I don't think that words could ever express how thankful I am for your contribution to my scholarship. It means a lot to me to know that there are people like you who care about the lives of young people.

In closing, I would like to thank you again for making my scholarship possible! I will stay in touch with you and keep you up to date with my education. If you would like to know more about me, feel free to inquire. Also, I would love to get to know you better.

With many thanks,

Kristin D. Dew

CHAPTER 15

Chapter Fifteen...Impact Player Partners Rodeo

During the spring of 2005, the rain soaked the central plains of Texas. Champion Ranch had seen more than its share of rainfall for the year. The grass was greener and thicker than ever and the cattle grazed like children at an ice cream parlor. The rodeo arena at Champion Ranch was almost ready. The new bleachers had been added to the south end of the arena. Twelve portable bathrooms had been donated to the event. The sales arena doors were open to accommodate the women, who held a violent aversion to porta-potties. A flatbed truck was rolled into place and served as a stage for the upcoming event. Special guest, performing artist Red Stegall was getting ready at the guesthouse next to the main house on Dick's ranch. Red would perform between rounds of the two round bull riding event.

The cowboy bunkhouse sat up on a hill overlooking the rodeo arena on Champion Ranch. Behind the arena spanned the expanse of Champion Ranch, a four star Picasso painting of the wind swept Champion prairies, cattle dogs chasing wandering steers and beet red sunrises climbing over the tree lined acres. Michael Wallrath, as the story goes, stood on the hill overlooking the rodeo arena recently. A ranch cowboy stood next to him. The view was spectacular. An early spring thunderstorm gave way to a lazy afternoon, draped in glistening streams of stunning yellow sunlight. A massive rainbow had risen from the eastern boundaries of the ranch. The rainbow climbed high into the sky and dropped down, off the horizon near the roadside fence line of Champion Ranch. The two men stood speechless and marveled at the exquisite colors exploding in the Texas sky. Finally, the young ranch cowboy looked at Dick Wallrath's oldest son and spoke.

"Hey, why don't we ride down to where that rainbow ends and really find out if there is a pot of gold down there?" The young cowboy asked.

"This is Champion Ranch. The pot of gold on this property is the property. My father has already found the pot of gold here." Michael smiled.

Saturday May 14, 2005 was the date scheduled for the first Impact Player Partners Rodeo at Champion Ranch. The Impact Player Partners is a nonprofit organization consisting of business leaders, athletes, entertainers and sports franchises dedicated to providing continuous emotional, career, and financial support to American military personnel who are severely wounded or disabled due to serving all Americans in the War on Terror. The mid-May rodeo was underwritten by Dick Wallrath and all the proceeds would be going to the Impact Player Partners. The event was scheduled to be a two round bull riding event with a third round short-go to determine first, second and third place. Red Stegall would perform between the first and second rounds. A complete country barbecue would follow the rodeo conclusion. The tickets sold to the event cost $25.00. The rodeo producer, his production costs, the catered meal, the event beverages, the golf carts used to transport spectators and special guests, the prize money for the competitors, the bullfighters, the rodeo clown, the announcer, the flag horse and flag girl were all underwritten by Dick Wallrath. Red Stegall's appearance fee was the only cost assumed by the ticket revenues. The Champion Ranch Impact Player Partners Benefit Rodeo raised nearly $20,000 for the Impact Player Partners.

Jerry Don Galloway produced the rodeo. Jerry has been a lifelong cowboy and is a member of the Hollywood Stuntman Hall of Fame. Jerry was a professional rodeo clown and bullfighter for fourteen years. Jerry is from Fort Worth, Texas and now leases the Yellow Rose Rodeo arena in Leona, Texas from Dick Wallrath. Jerry is a PRCA Rodeo

Producer and plays to host to more than twenty rodeos per year at the Yellow Rose. Jerry was hired to produce the Impact Player Partners Rodeo for Champion Ranch and Dick Wallrath. Twenty bulls and eighteen bull riders were brought in for the May 14 event. Many of the bulls were provided by Vernon Guidry. The Guidry Stock Contractors have an association with many of the top bucking bull bloodline organizations. Groups like White Water Skoal and Houdini provide top bucking bulls for the PBR and the PRCA. The twenty bulls brought to Champion Ranch on May 14 were top caliber professional bucking bulls. Many of the same bulls would end up bucking at PBR events later during the year. Some may eventually find their way to the PBR Finals, held each year in Las Vegas in early November or the PRCA Wrangler NFR held in early December each year, also in Las Vegas.

The bull riders for the Champion Ranch IPP (Impact Player Partners) Rodeo came from the top amateur ranks in Texas. Of the eighteen riders asked to compete, they came from the CPRA (Cowboys Professional Rodeo Association), the UPRA (United Professional Rodeo Association) and San Houston College in Huntsville, Texas. Dustin Richards, the 2004 CPRA Champion Bull Rider would eventually finish second at the Impact Player Partners rodeo.

The weather report had called for more than a fifty-percent chance of rain. The weather was perfect on Saturday morning, May 14. The guests began arriving around noon for the two o'clock event. A steady stream of vehicles were led from the main gates, down the two and a half miles of ranch roads to the rodeo arena. Golf carts and volunteers were on hand to transport anyone needing assistance. The golf carts were also on hand to transport the twelve injured veterans, invited to the event as the guests of honor. Coolers were set up every few feet to provide beverages for the guests. Mike Wells, the President of the Houston Stock Show and Rodeo arrived early. Sid Steiner, the 2002 World Champion Steer Wrestler was on hand to lend his support. Many, who could not attend for one reason or another, sent checks in regardless.

The bulls waited patiently in two equal sized holding pens adjacent to the chutes. Some worked leisurely to establish their space within the holding pens. Some stared blankly at the arriving guests. No movement precluded the ferocity of the event and the danger to the participants. There are seven events at most major rodeos. The last event is always bull riding. The draw has always been the extreme danger of the competition and the fearless resolve of the competitors. In past decade, the PBR has exceeded even the most optimistic predictions for success. The PRCA followed with the X-treme Bulls Tour. The popularity of bull riding has never been higher. The bucking bull breeding business has exploded. Bulls have never been stronger, meaner or more athletic. The bulls brought to Champion Ranch on May 14 were no exception. The event began on schedule.

The rodeo announcer was able to settle the crowd. A single paint horse rode into the arena. The horse was ridden by a young girl, no more than ten years old. She carried an American flag in one hand and held the reins lightly with her other hand. The flag rose high above the animal and rider. The young girl led the black and white paint horse around the outer edges of the inner arena. The horse began slowly and the flag draped gently toward the arena floor. The audience waited for the national anthem to begin. The music started slowly, but the anthem was not played first. Toby Kieth's, Courtesy of the Red, White and Blue began to rumble through the public address system. The music was loud and the notes were crystal clear. The girl and her paint horse began to step up the pace. The flag rolled a bit with the wind. The music was cranked up another notch. The familiar verses rolled from everyone's lips.

Uncle Sam put your name at the top of his list,

And the Statue of Liberty started shakin her fist...

The paint horse and the young girl were at full speed. The flag flew perfectly horizontal as the horse raced around the arena at a tremendous pace. The young girl never wavered in the saddle. She rode like she was part of the horse. They worked in symmetrical harmony, as goose bumps rolled up and down the arms of all in attendance. The song closed and the young girl and her paint horse rolled to a halt. The flag settled and everyone remained standing. The national anthem followed. Only in Texas, can a national sentiment stand toe to toe with tradition. The audience ovation was genuine and long. Twelve wounded veterans stood as well.

Two rounds of bull riding left no doubt about the difficulty to stay aboard an eighteen hundred pound time bomb for eight seconds. The young men in the competition averaged under twenty-one years of age. Red Stegall recalled another era of Texas cowboys in song and verse. A mountain of brisket and ribs disappeared after the competition. The young bull riders nursed black and purple bruises, pulled muscles, dislocated joints and trampled egos. The bulls came out on top for the day. Dick Wallrath shook the hands of each veteran guest. They all spent time together after the rodeo. The first Impact Player Partners Rodeo, hosted by Champion Ranch and Dick Wallrath was a success, but by no means an end. Dick Wallrath held his first benefit rodeo as much to raise funds as to learn from the event. The American commitment to the War on Terror will go on for years. The military sacrifice and determination to complete the job will lead to many more debilitating injuries and many more making the ultimate sacrifice. The need to assist those willing to give so much to our country will not fade away soon. Neither will the efforts from Dick Wallrath. Mr. Wallrath's extended hand will not only reach those who cannot afford an education, it will reach those poised to delay an education in order to defend our nation.

IMPACT PLAYER HALL OF FAME...CLASS OF 2005

The Impact Player Hall of Fame is designed to honor those individuals who have reached for all encompassing excellence in their life. In particular, inductees display a laser focus on serving others before self. Dr. Richard Traum is the first Impact Player Hall of Fame inductee. Dr. Traum was the first leg amputee to run a marathon and is the founder of the Achilles Track Club.

The Impact Player Hall of Fame also honors those military men and women (and their families) who have been severely wounded or killed in the War on Terror by providing emotional support through a forum of public appreciation. Funds raised support our severely wounded military heroes via Impact Player Partners, a 501 c 3 organization that provides emotional, career and financial assistance.

The Impact Player Hall of Fame, Class of 2005 is a gathering of extraordinary individuals who have consistently displayed the exceptional power of the human spirit. The world is a better place because of their actions in life.*

President George Herbert Walker Bush	Danielle Green
Dom Capers	Andrew Houghton
Roger Clemens	Mike McNaughton
Ben Crenshaw	Thomas Parr and Joannie Parr
A. O. Bum Phillips	David Robinson
Roger Staubach	Pat Tillman

*...Impact Player Partners Event Guide 2005, www.impactplayer.org

George Bush

April 2005

Dear Dick,

I am honored to be in the company of Pat Tillman, a true hero, Dom Capers, Ben Crenshaw and Danielle Green as one of the 2005 Impact Player Hall of Fame inductees.

I have the feeling none of us can do enough for our nation's military, but organizations like Impact Player Partners do an outstanding job of making sure those who serve and those who are injured in the line of duty know that all Americans are grateful for their service to the country.

Please convey to all inductees including Dom Capers, Ben Crebshaw and Danielle Green my congratulations on this well-deserved honor; and of course, we all remember Pat Tillman in our prayers and with gratitude in our hearts.

Barbara joins me in sending warmest wishes for a memorable celebration of American patriotism and heroism.

Sincerely,

George H. W. Bush**

Mr. Dick Lynch

Founder and President

Impact Player Partners

P. O. Box 531201

Cincinnati, Ohio 45253

**...received from the office of Dick Lynch to the office of Dick Wallrath, 2005

CHAPTER 16

Chapter Sixteen...Personal Inventory, Carry the Message to Others

Dick Wallrath: Hello, my name is Dick. I'm an ex-drunk and a recovered alcoholic. I'm sober again today and today makes roughly 13,675 days, but who's counting?

There are no absolute predictable patterns to determine the next alcoholic, the next cancer victim or the next stroke victim. The foreseeable nature of the medical science industry is a reactive organization. There have been great strides taken over the past twenty years to educate the public on sensible measures to reduce the likelihood of many debilitating diseases. The ability to predict and prevent alcoholism, cancer or most life-threatening diseases is not unlike the analogy of the federal and local police departments. Steven Spielberg produced a movie recently called *Minority Report*. In that movie, the police were able to predict murders and subsequently arrested the potential perpetrator prior to the actual murder. The concept made for an intriguing story line, but the foundation was purely fluff. Choices are not always the definitive link between health and illness. Lou Gerhig did not choose to contract Amyotrophic Lateral Sclerosis (ALS) during the absolute prime of his baseball career. Mr. Gerhig would have much preferred to look at a hard slider or an inside fastball than to face those microphones and cameras at Yankee Stadium on the day he delivered the infamous "I am the luckiest man on the face of the earth" speech. Lance Armstrong did not choose to contract cancer. He was an accomplished athlete, ate properly, did not smoke and could have easily been placed in the lowest percentile to contract cancer. Dina Denise Wallrath lived a healthy lifestyle. She, meticulously, watched her caloric intake, made a conscious effort on a daily basis to provide a healthy example for her family, exercised regularly and contracted one of the deadliest forms of lymphoma. Deede did not choose to contract cancer. Alcoholism is a disease and the choice to abstain

211

from alcohol is often an option that has arrived too late.

The Twelve Step Program has been the foundation for success to people worldwide. There is a fine line to draw between the anonymity that has been the cornerstone of the program's mantra and the potential to reach so many more by the documentation of personal triumph. For the purpose of relating the life experiences of Dick Wallrath and the importance that the Twelve Step Program has had on Mr. Wallrath's recovery, the message carried throughout this chapter will be pulled from generic locales and nameless individuals. Mr. Wallrath will always respect and live by the Twelve Steps and the Twelve Traditions. The Twelfth Tradition states, "Anonymity is the spiritual foundation of all our Traditions, ever reminding us to place principles before personalities."

The first principle of success in life has to be the acknowledgement that success is attainable. Every person in the Twelve Step Program can achieve success if they become aware of the program and make themselves available to what the guidelines dictate. Again, the simplicity of the program is evasive. The only requirement for membership is the desire to stop drinking. Success within the program is not a singular achievement.

Dick Wallrath: I wanted to be sober more than anything in the world, but I drank every single day. It was right in front of me and I still couldn't find the sonofabitch. I figured that I could do it my way and I figured wrong for three years. I drank like a fool for fifteen years, joined the program and drank for another three years until the boat finally stopped rockin. The damn thing is not for people, who need to stop drinking, the program is for people who want to stop drinking. The notion that I should, I should, I should will get you nowhere. When you want to stop your destruction is the only timeline that will work. All that was asked of me was to stop drinking for the day. Remember, if I did not drink for that one day, then no way in hell was I going to get drunk. The simplicity kicks you in the ass every day. Worry about the present. Nobody promised you tomorrow, so don't get all bent out of shape about it. We worry about each day as it greets us. Hell, I need a partner for solitaire, but I figured this one out. I have seen many people walk out of the meetings and start drinking again. Some made it back and many more didn't. I never met anyone who came running back to tell us that they figured out a way to drink and still follow the program.

There's the old story of the village idiot. He watched the town blacksmith pound out the iron horseshoes each day. The blacksmith would take the red-hot iron spheres and toss them into the grass to cool down. The village idiot walked over to the pile of horseshoes one day and picked one up. He dropped it almost immediately. The blacksmith shook his head and asked rhetorically, "pretty hot, huh?" The village idiot shook his hand and replied, "No, it doesn't take me long to look at a horseshoe."

We all have some instincts to avoid the obvious. The Twelve Step Program has no shortcuts and no hidden agendas. The success is based within its simplicity.

The meeting halls are often empty office buildings. The industrial parks are vacant. The parking lots are virtually empty. Custodial details can be seen through the windows. The mirrored glass is dark. A side door to the office complex is open. A dozen people gather outside to smoke cigarettes. They greet each other with warm hugs. Many carry trays of food. It is birthday night. Birthday celebrations are held each month. Usually, they are held on the last Friday of the month. Sobriety is celebrated on a yearly basis. At any given meeting, there can be 150 years of sobriety in attendance. One man may have 20 years of sobriety under his belt. Another may have 16 years of sobriety. Still another, may be celebrating his first year of sobriety or his first month of sobriety. A dinner buffet is laid out. At the recreational lounge bar, there is coffee, Mountain Dew and plenty of Red Bull. The smokers watch the clock. Eight o'clock is at hand.

The meetings begin with a call to order and a moment of silence. The serenity prayer is read aloud and in unison. The Twelve Steps and the Twelve Traditions are read aloud. A forty-two year old woman takes the podium. She has 14 years of sobriety conquered. She is comfortable at the microphone. The early days of her sobriety were much different. She announced her first name and her affliction. The group acknowledged her appearance.

Jane Doe I: To thine own self be true. There is no problem so great that a drink will not make it worse. I love that line. I came into this program kicking and screaming. I had attempted suicide and failed. Apparently, God had a different plan for me. I like to think that way because the alternative was bleak. After failing at everything else in life, so I gave in to the ultimate failure and tried to kill myself. Lo and behold, I failed at that, too. I prefer to believe that God had other plans for me. I have a ten-year old daughter that is proof of that…the program has worked miracles for me and I know one thing for certain. I could not have accomplished any of these things in my life without the people in this room. You are everything to me and I owe my life and my daughter's life to everyone here tonight.

John Doe I: (two years sober) I became reachable and teachable. I would still like to drink, but bad things continue to happen to me when I drink. Sober is safer and hope is much better than jail.

John Doe II: (seventeen years sober) Hell, I never thought I would live this long, much less be sober for this long. I have a huge family before my eyes. I have friends who are dead because of alcohol and friends who are in prison because they could not control their demons. Its' all about progress, not perfection. Progress is staying sober today. Perfection is down the road and I can't go there just yet. I may never go there. I seem to be doing pretty good with progress.

The variety of people in each meeting is staggering. The bank account doesn't matter to the program. Wherever a Twelve Step meeting is held, in any part of the nation or the world, the members new and old may include some unemployed alcoholics, a few construction workers, or a waitress. The meetings may also include a bartender, a shoe salesman, a retail cashier, a corporate CEO, a bank president, an attorney, more than one physician, a surgeon, a pediatrician, an auto mechanic or a mortician. The job application for the program does not have a space for experience required, gender or race. Alcoholism does not discriminate based on gender, color, creed or religion. It is safe to say that the bottle has never refused an African American, a Jewish man, a Muslim or a woman. Another birthday meeting begins somewhere. The members load up their plates and save room for the two dozen dessert trays that line the dessert tables.

John Doe III: (eight years sober) I started out with six years of going to meetings with liquor on my breath. I wasn't kidding anyone but myself. I used to drink so much when I was younger that

215

I actually woke up one day in another state and I had no idea of where I was, how I got there or what set of circumstances occurred to place me where I was. I gave up two wives and three children to my drinking. By the time I got sober, I had missed so much of their lives that I didn't think I could ever find a way back to them. I had so many bad days, but the worst day of my life was the day I thought I had lost my spirituality. That was ten times worse than drinking. Who knows what triggers the resentment to success? Bad things happen in life. Bad times and tragedies are not reserved for the alcoholic. Recovered alcoholics, non-drinkers and model citizens have tragic things occur in their lives. Our troubles return when we use those tragedies to pop back into the old loop. My first son was killed in an automobile accident two years after I stopped drinking. I was a mess. I swore at God more than I swore at my old high school football coach. I used something completely out of my control to facilitate my path right back to the bar I used to live at. I used the loss of my son to give me a reason to drink again and that loss also gave me a reason to prove to everyone else that there was no God. Something stopped me. I know that my son had a hand in whatever made me return to this program. The Twelve Step Program brought me back to my God and my spirituality. It brought me back to my children and gave me a new wife. I now have a new son and a new grandson, at the same time. God had another plan for me. I have been chosen to live a blessed life. I don't know why I was chosen, but I do intend to spend every day of the rest of my life giving my children and grandchildren a reason to stand next to me. I will spend every day of my life giving my wife a reason to be proud of the name she took from me. I had to come to this program to find out what my higher power had in store for me.

Dick Wallrath doesn't walk around with a scarlet "A" tattooed to his forehead. The success of the Twelve Step Program is not rooted within the pages of a manuscript or the blackboards of a vacant office somewhere. The success of the program must begin with the humility in each member or potential member to acknowledge a power greater than himself. Without that, there will be no success. The concept of anonymity within the program is essential to the complete recovery. To embrace the personal victories and understand how they may relate to others is not the loss of anonymity but the expansion of opportunity. Dick Wallrath still speaks to many Twelve Step programs throughout Texas. When a man with 37 years of sobriety takes the podium, the normally chatty members get quiet in a hurry. When a new member had his last drink a month ago and a man with 37 years of sobriety is going to tell him how to live his life without alcohol, he shuts his mouth and listens to every word. Dick Wallrath doesn't attend meetings to speak in polite cliches. Dick Wallrath couldn't care less if you got offended by some nasty words during his time at the podium. He will tell his peers that the world does not owe them anything. Dick will announce to everyone in the room that the time is at hand to take responsibility for the actions of your past, alter the direction and nature of those actions and find someone or something that will touch your soul and never let go. Dick Wallrath will never finish an address without relating a poem that has defined his success for all of those 37 years of sobriety:

The Touch of the Masters Hand

Twas battered and scarred and the auctioneer

Thought it scarcely worth his while to waste much time on the old violin,

But he held it up with a smile;

"What am I bidden, good folks, " he cried,

"Who'll start the bidden for me? A dollar, a dollar, then two."

"Only two? Two dollars, who'll make it three? Three dollars, once,

three dollars twice, going for three."

But no, from the room, far back a gray-haired man came forward and picked up the bow.

Then wiping the dust from the old violin and tightening the loose strings,

He played a melody pure and sweet as caroling angels sings.

The music ceased and the auctioneer with a voice that was quiet and low, said,

"What am I bid for the old violin?" And he held it up with the bow.

"A thousand dollars, and who'll make it two? Two thousand? And who'll make it three?"

"Three thousand once, three thousand twice and going and gone," said he.

The people cheered but some of them cried,

"We do not understand what changed its worth." Swift came the reply:

The touch of the master's hand.

And many a man with life out of tune, and battered and scarred with sin,

Is auctioned cheap to the thoughtless crowd, much like the old violin,

A mess of pottage, a glass of wine, a game and he travels on.

He is going once and going twice. He's going and almost gone.

But the Master comes, and the foolish crowd never can quite understand

The worth of a soul and the change that is wrought

By the touch of the Master's hand.

Myra Brooks Welch

Dick Wallrath: There are times to make a difference in someone's life. I'm not certain which end of the escalator is going to be waiting for me when the bus pulls up, but this second half of my life has been a hell of a lot more fun than the first half. Hell, if I knew that the best high in the world came from giving back something that was a gift in the first place, then I never would have wasted so much time trying to get high from anything as artificial as some stale ass whiskey. This country is full of people to look up to and full of people that can carve the word "Hero" on their own headstone. My legacy is not about what I leave behind. My legacy will be about what I did when I got here. I guess I got in foul trouble during the first half of the game. My coach pulled my ass out of the game until I wrapped my brain around what was important about the game. I found the master's hand and he pointed me back into the game. He gave me the ball and I ran with it. I'm going to continue to do the best I can with what I've got. In the end, I will look at my children and my grandchildren and tell them to cherish every holiday and every insignificant moment together. I missed those moments and as I grow older and wiser, I know those memories are not frozen in the back of my mind. They are not hidden in yellow photographs buried with an old uniform that doesn't fit. I never stop wondering why it took me so long to determine the direction my life was meant to take. That is a question that has no answer. Maybe I will know someday, but I cannot escape the gratitude that fills my life because the direction DID change. I have one man to answer to each day. I can look him in the eye each morning and he will know that I did everything in my power yesterday to become a better person. That man is in my mirror. When I cannot look him in the eye each morning, then God will send my bus to come get me. Until then, I have some unfinished business with a whole bunch of young people. Some I know and some I have never met and never will. There was a high price paid for God to give me the opportunities that he gave me. I will do my best not to miss a single installment on the road to restitution. This journey was never about me.

Afterword...

I have been very fortunate to spend a great deal of time in Texas over the past three years. Two books and some big Lone Star mileage have brought me to some pragmatic conclusions. While most of my time was spent shuffling from Dallas to Fort Worth, to Austin, to San Antonio, to Houston and up to Centerville, I veered off to visit Waco, Bastrop, Stephenville, San Marcos, New Braunfels, Galveston, Lubbock, Madisonville, Normangee and Huntsville. I am from Chicago and I spend part of each year in Cave Creek, Arizona. During my fifty-one years on the planet, I have lived in seven different states and I have spent time in every state in the union except Alaska. I have never heard anyone proclaim the vainglory declarations about their state of residence like a Texan. I have lived in or near Chicago for decades and I have never heard one neighbor, associate, business partner, literary subject or friend trumpet the desire to close every road, airport, bus terminal or bicycle path in order to leave Illinois alone. Hell, I cannot recall an Illinois politician that ran a campaign from a grass roots theme of Illinois pride. I cannot tell you what is on the state flag of Illinois. I can tell you what is on the state flag of Texas! I do not recall the state symbol of Illinois plastered on any briefcase, mailbox, vehicle bumper, ball cap, belt buckle, bedroom ceiling, or dinner plate. I do recall the Texas Star imprinted on everything that I just mentioned, as well as men's and women's jewelry to clothing lines to the upholstery in a Ford F150 pick-up truck. Texans like their state and they are not shy about conveying that information to anyone. Dick Wallrath is proud to be a Texan. He wears his state on his sleeve like a soldier dons the Army uniform or a sailor straightens the buttercup white hat on his head. With all of his Texas pride and believe me, there is plenty, Dick Wallrath is most proud of the work he has done with Texas young people.

Dick does not spend his time shopping for the next Gulfstream Lear Jet to roll off the assembly line. Air travel is simply a commercial coach ticket. He doesn't drag a sixty-foot yacht to the numerous lakes in Texas. His home, while beautiful, is not the palace that belies someone of his financial status. He drives a Chevy Silverado pick-up around town and when the trips call for Houston or Austin, he drives a white Escalade truck with Champion Ranch emblazoned on the door panels. There are no Bentleys or Mercedes sedans. Dick spends his money on big-ass steers and those purchases translate into college scholarship money for young people who may not get the chance to attend college. Dick Wallrath gives money directly to the FFA and 4-H organizations that will serve to establish permanent scholarship funds that will live on long after Mr. Wallrath caught his bus. These scholarship funds will be funded with millions of dollars. Mr. Wallrath will continue to assist the fund raising efforts of the Impact Player Partners and through their combined efforts, the money and awareness directed to our returning injured veterans will climb steadily. Dick Wallrath believes there is no greater calling than the unselfish sacrifice to defend this nation. Mr. Wallrath does not lend lip service to his passion. Dick Wallrath puts his money and his actions where his big old Texas passion lies.

There are lessons in every phase of our lives. At fifty-one, I continue to learn from each new project, each new book and each new subject who is gracious enough to allow me into their lives. The Texas lesson that has jumped off the pages of this book and slapped me around like a Herculean nanny on steroids, is the lesson of action. Critics take apart everything. They find a calling in the dissection of what it is that they have never been able to accomplish with action. Personally, I have never been able to understand criticism, as a career path. There are simply some actions that do not have agendas. There are simply some actions that have direct positive results. There are simply some actions that do not need to be analyzed. There are simply some actions that skip the traditional roads of imaginary cost ledgers and beeline directly to the actual beneficiary. These are the actions of Dick Wallrath.

The definition of redemption is the act of redeeming, i.e. to make good by performing, to atone for, to be free from the consequence of sin. Before we leave Champion Ranch and Mr. Wallrath, let me examine the adage…*to be free from the consequence of sin.* I believe there is no human being capable of assessing who among us is to be judged…free from the consequence of sin. What is assessable is the effort to seek personal redemption and the tangible result from the effort. Dick Wallrath did some bad things in his life. He will be the first one to sit down and explain them to you. Candid is not a concept that Mr. Wallrath has avoided. The journey to accept the past, deal with the issues revealed and to turn those lessons into something much more is the way to begin to understand Richard Wallrath.

Men like Mr. Wallrath are fashionable targets and easy prey for those critics who will never accept the notion that true generosity is not the narcissistic extension of wealth. The only true gauge of philanthropy is to become the subject. There are too many detractors willing to examine the actions of so few. I recall the boxing promoter (a.k.a. Don King type), ranting at a pre-fight press conference. "We will prevail tomorrow night!" Exactly how many punches will the promoter throw and how many will he absorb? How many hours has the promoter spent in the gym? How many miles has he run at 6:00 a.m.? Zero. It has always been much easier to review the action than to initiate the action. Critics are like small town carnival rides. They don't cost much, but you're always disappointed when they're done. The young people of Texas are very grateful that every so often, there are men and women who step out from under the blanket of cheap talk, and commit to something that neither requires the mantle of adulation or the circuit of coronation. There are such things as good deeds. They may be simple and small or they may be encompassing and everlasting. Regardless, these actions get the job done. Dick Wallrath has gotten the job done.

General Patton said, "Lead me, follow me or get out of my way!" Not many were about to lead a man like General Patton. Multitudes of people were destined to follow the eccentric leader. Those on the sidelines, content as spectators or too timid to participate, were best advised to step back. In Texas, those descriptions are Richard "Dick" Wallrath.

James Pomerantz

Acknowledgments…

…To the young people of Texas, who have sought to earn their way in life.

…To the young men and women of the military, who have taught us about honor, courage and commitment.

…To the Wallrath family, Patsy Murphy, Gary and Alexander Robertson, who showed strength, compassion and understanding.

…To Dick Wallrath, keep 'er going! Don't expect that bus to stop anytime soon.

…To my family, when I pursue life with passion and purpose, I am a better man. Thank you for understanding what it is that makes me function and not asking me to change. Mary, Jimmy, Kiley, Michael and Matthew…I love you.

.